Elements in Translation and Interpreting
edited by
Kirsten Malmkjær
University of Leicester

RISK MANAGEMENT IN TRANSLATION

Anthony Pym
Universitat Rovira i Virgili

Shaftesbury Road, Cambridge CB2 8EA, United Kingdom

One Liberty Plaza, 20th Floor, New York, NY 10006, USA

477 Williamstown Road, Port Melbourne, VIC 3207, Australia

314–321, 3rd Floor, Plot 3, Splendor Forum, Jasola District Centre, New Delhi – 110025, India

103 Penang Road, #05–06/07, Visioncrest Commercial, Singapore 238467

Cambridge University Press is part of Cambridge University Press & Assessment, a department of the University of Cambridge.

We share the University's mission to contribute to society through the pursuit of education, learning and research at the highest international levels of excellence.

www.cambridge.org
Information on this title: www.cambridge.org/9781009546843

DOI: 10.1017/9781009546836

© Anthony Pym 2025

This publication is in copyright. Subject to statutory exception and to the provisions of relevant collective licensing agreements, no reproduction of any part may take place without the written permission of Cambridge University Press & Assessment.

When citing this work, please include a reference to the DOI 10.1017/9781009546836

First published 2025

A catalogue record for this publication is available from the British Library

ISBN 978-1-009-54684-3 Hardback
ISBN 978-1-009-54687-4 Paperback
ISSN 2633-6480 (online)
ISSN 2633-6472 (print)

Cambridge University Press & Assessment has no responsibility for the persistence or accuracy of URLs for external or third-party internet websites referred to in this publication and does not guarantee that any content on such websites is, or will remain, accurate or appropriate.

Risk Management in Translation

Elements in Translation and Interpreting

DOI: 10.1017/9781009546836
First published online: January 2025

Anthony Pym
Universitat Rovira i Virgili

Author for correspondence: Anthony Pym, anthony.pym@urv.cat

Abstract: Once fidelity and equivalence are abandoned, how can successful translation be understood? Risk management offers an alternative way of looking at the work of translators and their social function. It posits that the greater the cultural differences, the greater the risks of failed communication. What can be done to manage those risks? Drawing on the ways translators and interpreters handle intercultural encounters by adjusting what is said, this Element outlines a series of strategies that can be applied to all kinds of cross-cultural communication. Practical examples are drawn from a wide range of contexts, from Australian bushfires to court interpreting in Barcelona, with special regard for the new kinds of risks presented by machine translation and generative AI. The result is a critical view of the professionalization of translation, and a fresh account of democratized translation as a rich human activity in the service of cross-cultural cooperation.

This element has a video abstract available at: Cambridge.org/EITI_Pym

Keywords: translation, risk management, cooperation, trust, translation technologies

© Anthony Pym 2025

ISBNs: 9781009546843 (HB), 9781009546874 (PB), 9781009546836 (OC)
ISSNs: 2633-6480 (online), 2633-6472 (print)

Contents

1 Why Talk about Risk? 1
2 Risk of What? 8
3 Types of Risk Management 18
4 Trust as Risk Management 31
5 Risks in Automated Translation 38
6 A Case for More Risk-Taking 50
  References 58

1 Why Talk about Risk?

Risk management is something translators – the term here includes interpreters – are always doing, along with anyone who works between cultures, and in fact anyone who communicates. People who communicate between cultures tend to manage risks more consciously than many others because, in general, there is less certainty in the frontier spaces: we know less about the people we are talking with; the multiplicity of languages compounds the complexity of each language; we are less familiar with expected procedures; we are less likely to trust fully the people we communicate with; they are more likely to distrust us. Those greater uncertainties are good reasons for talking about how translators manage risks.

A second reason is more philosophical. Much thinking on translation, at least in the Western traditions, assumes the ideal of a perfect translation. The words for that ideal have changed over the centuries, from *fidelity* to *adequacy* to *equivalence* to *accuracy*, but all those terms assume that the aim of a translation is to reproduce something from the previous text – the better the reproduction, the more ideal the translation. Risk, on that view, would be the probability of misrepresentation, of the translator making a linguistic mistake. And avoiding risk would involve things like training more, paying more attention, checking more, or generally working harder. On that view, more effort will bring you closer to the ideal representation by reducing uncertainty. That is a very common way of thinking about translation, and an unfortunately common mainstay of translation pedagogy.

I do not share that view. This is not because I shun hard work – not that I seek it either. It is because I do not believe there is just one ideal translation. Or rather, if there happens to be just one possible translation of a given sentence, a translation that everyone agrees is much better than all others, then that certitude concerns areas of terminology or grammar that are imposed by an external authority, perhaps the Microsoft glossary or the institutional powers that decide what correct grammar is. For the parts of translation that are of interest to me here, the problems of translating a text do not have clear, simple solutions. They require interpretation. And since different people interpret in different ways, there are many possible solutions to a translation problem and no infallible rule-based way of deciding between those solutions. Try it for yourself: translate a longish sentence, then retranslate it as many ways as you can, then attempt to say why your first translation should be the only one that fits some kind of ideal. If the experiment *does* give just one ideal translation, do a few more sentences, and make sure they are really complex! In sum, for the translation problems that concern me here, there is no such thing as an ideal solution, no matter how much popular belief continues to accept and circulate that ideal.

Once you accept that view, risk is not just the probability that an error might be made. It becomes a way of explaining how translators can work, communicate, and be trusted in situations where there is no absolute certainty. Part of that is news to no one: many people tell us that interpretation is necessary, transformations are everywhere, translation is creative, and so on. With apologies, here I would like to say something a little less empty and hopefully more useful and precise. For me, the great attraction of risk management is that it enables an account of translation that does *not* require ideals of fixed, stable meaning, and yet can still explain part of what translators do, can do so empirically, and can also help in their training.

How can we avoid the facile ideals? The first step is to insist that risk is the probability not just of misrepresentation but more generally of the entire communication act failing in some way. Once you take that step, risk becomes something more than a particular set of hazards. Risks can also be mitigated, transferred, or taken on in the hope of achieving communicative rewards. That is one very good reason for talking about them. You can do different things with them, as opposed to the basic language error that is only right or wrong.

This Is Not Particularly about Running a Business

What is risk? It is the probability of failure. That is a standard view, found in economics, psychology, sociology, and a hundred other places, right through to pandemic control and climate-change science. Here, though, the failure is specifically in cross-cultural communication, and more specifically in failures to reach the kinds of understandings needed for cooperation (on which, more later). The point to make now, so as not to disappoint anyone, is that I am *not* offering lessons in how to run a translation business, as can certainly be done (Stoeller 2003; Lammers 2011; Canfora & Ottmann 2015, 2018). Good communication will hopefully lead to good business, but there are a few even more interesting ways in which the two sides can be related.

I am concerned with the way translation decisions are made in situations of uncertainty, then with the strategies that orient those decisions, and then with ways the strategies of participants meet in a communication act. The one set of concepts should be able to follow those steps from the cognitive to the social. That requires more than business. The business kind of risk has to do with numbers: profits and losses are quantifiable reductions of uncertainty. But risk is also a set of psychological and social constructs and dispositions, operating at the levels of intuition and ideology more than in any careful numerical calculations. Confronted with several ways of rendering a problematic sentence, translators intuitively assess the effects that each solution will have on the imagined receiver, just as they subconsciously assess the ways those choices will fit in with the translation interaction as a whole. Their innate emotional responses might be seen as embodiments of successful risk-management decisions over millennia of evolution (Harari 2016: 391), but the translators are not particularly thinking like the economic subject – the rational egoist – that runs a good business. They do not have numbers flashing in their mind. Yet they are managing risks nonetheless.

As an example, I will have quite a lot to say about a high-stakes message in Australia telling people that a bushfire is approaching and it is too late for them to leave their homes – although risk management is by no means limited to such extreme cases. The addressees must prepare for the fire, quickly. As I translate the text, I wonder whether to reproduce the second person *you*, as in 'It is too late for *you* to leave.' In contemporary behavior-change messages in English, that second person is normal enough. It is actually recommended in most guidelines, so I should probably use it. But if I am translating into Japanese, the passive is more normal, so I might decide to get rid of the second person: 'It is too late to leave.' And in Chinese, having many short sentences with 'you' does not sound authoritative enough, so the receivers may not take the message seriously. And then, if I am preparing a text to be machine-translated into many languages, given that everyone has to understand this message and the fire is advancing fast, I might delete the second person altogether, given that it is likely to create problems down the line. Many languages make distinctions between the formal and informal (*tu* vs. *vous* in French, *tú* vs. *usted* in Spanish, *du* vs. *Sie* in German, εσύ vs. εσείς in Greek, 你 vs. 您 in Chinese) and machine translations rarely make consistent selections between the two. All those possible risks can flash through my mind, none of them based on any numerical calculations but all of them constituting certain estimated likelihoods of failure, felt as consequences that it might be good to avoid. On the basis of accumulated experience or recycled collective imaginings, the risks have thereby become psychological constructs that are accorded more or less weight in the decision-making process. And then, once I settle on the idea that the form of the second person is rather unlikely to affect the actual understanding of the message and that what counts more is the speed of the translation because the fire is approaching, I could just leave as many second persons as there are in the existing text, accepting the risks in the interests of urgency – I let machine translation do its work and pray for the best. What would you do? (Remember, the fire is approaching fast.)

Although such decisions are rarely based on any exact calculations, the numbers can sometimes come later. For example, probabilities are calculated on the basis of past usage whenever translations enter the training data for machine translations or various forms of generative AI. Other times, there is a virtue in calculating them through research on how a specific text genre works linguistically in different languages. If you are in a hurry, you might go with the probabilities that are used in the algorithms of our automation systems, running risks that you cannot control but that have indeed been calculated in places we cannot see. Of course, if you have time, check them with a little research: gather a handful of parallel texts and contextual examples for each target language. A few meaningful numbers can help you make decisions with enhanced confidence, but without implying at any moment that the translating mind is a narrow rationalist.

Note that this is a matter of felt probabilities. When I use terms like 'high-stakes' and 'low-stakes' (for the estimated consequences of a choice) or 'high-risk' and 'low-risk' (for the degree of consequence plus the estimated frequency of occurrence), there are no simple binary oppositions at work. The probabilities locate any number of points between those named polarities.

There are, however, cases where a more business-oriented kind of risk management works against that interiorized, affective kind of probability, in fact against any personal confidence in translation decisions. Take, for instance, the fact that many subtitlers are required to work from a written script without seeing the actual film they are translating. Why? Because the logic of business says there is a high probability that the audiovisual file will be leaked into the public domain, which might eat into the company's profits. That is a numerical kind of risk. At the same time, it incurs the risk that the subtitlers' renditions will contradict what happens on the screen, or will be general, vague, and contain omissions – since those are the kinds of strategies subtitlers tend to employ when they cannot access the audiovisual information and are effectively flying blind. That second kind of risk, the kind that the blindfolded subtitlers must deal with, has no numbers associated with it, even though it is being managed through the subtitlers' risk-averse decisions. Similarly obscured are the kinds of losses thereby incurred to viewers' receptions of the translated film, hopefully with some financial consequences down the line. For as long as there are no numbers able to address questions about the risks taken in the production and reception of subtitles, the business practice will probably continue as if a publicly available audiovisual file were the only risk to be considered, in a situation of classical information asymmetry. A little empirical research, a simple comparison of reception processes with and without subtitlers being able to see the film, could hopefully show the companies some further numbers, given that numbers seem to be the only kind of language that could change a nefarious business practice. And those further numbers can come from researchers. This is one of the many areas in which research can intervene and help change the kind of risk management that is being applied.

Does that mean that the risk is actually in the numbers? Not at all. Risk is a creation of human minds when we try to decide between different courses of action. We *sense* the effect a subtitle might have, just as the film distributors – truth be told – *fear* uncontrolled release of the film more than can be justified by actual market numbers. Fansubbed versions of bootlegged films can generate public interest and thereby *enhance* commercial success – the classic case is how repeated copyright infringements created a market for Japanese anime in the United States (Leonard 2005). But what company directors fear most in translation is loss of control. Their decisions are at least as affective as they are numerical.

This Is Not about Everything Translators Think They Do

Risk management can help explain the ways translators solve problems, just as it can help translators think about how to solve problems more effectively or less instinctively. Of course, translators do many other things as well, and when they do those other things, they have no reason at all to consider risks or be concerned with managing them. When there are fixed grammatical rules and standard terminology, there is no strictly translational problem to solve: you apply the rules, obeying and reproducing authority. Or when a translator stays as close to the text as possible, following the author and making only the adjustments necessary to ensure the translation is comprehensible, they are probably not thinking in terms of risk management. That does not mean, however, that their activities cannot be *explained* in terms of risk management. When a translator applies authorities, playing it safe, the risk of communicative failure has implicitly been *transferred* to those authorities – don't blame me, blame the Microsoft glossary! And when a translator follows the text closely, there is also a certain transfer of responsibility to the original authors – they said it, not me! Risk management can offer explanations, even when the translator is not particularly aware of having any particular disposition to risk.

That is not to say that all risks are efficiently managed in the mind of the translator or simply intuited in the moment of production. In 1405, Leonardo Bruni complained that when something was good in his translation, all praise went to the author, and when something was bad, all blame went to the translator (Bruni 1405/1969). That tells us risk management is also happening in the minds of the people who *receive* the translations. Bruni claimed that this injustice was because only translators can see how much work is involved. Outsiders do not appreciate the fruits of those labors because they do not see the labors. If a little research can help show how much work is involved, or can hopefully change the way film companies treat subtitlers, the wider aim might be to change the way translations are received.

This Is Not Particularly about How to Be Rational

Frege thought that knowledge of different languages allowed people to somehow become more logical: "when we see that the same thought can be worded in different ways, our mind separates off the husk from the kernel. [...] This is how the differences between languages can facilitate our grasp of what is logical" (1979: 6). The idea implies that logic is common to all languages. If you get the logic right, all you have to do is express it in whatever language you are working into. That should make translators the most rational people in the world! Yet Frege's was an external vision, like the readers who did not see or appreciate Bruni's labors as a translator or the subtitlers who cannot see what is happening in the film. The more information the translator can find, and the more information we obtain on the mind of the translating translator, the less we can assume that there is any pure logic at work. As for the thing to be translated, it can be anything from a price to an emotion, a linguistic function, a pragmatic effect, a semantic unit, a gesture, or anything in accordance with the purpose of the communication. There is no pure logic to be found there.

The question is important because the dominant models of risk management tend to assume a logic of rational calculations, especially in neoclassical economics, where there are not only numbers but also clear concepts to which the numbers are supposed to be attached. Risk, on that view, is often calculated as the uncertainty of a fixed expectation, as in ISO 31000:2018 on risk management (Section 3.1). For me, working with language translation, the assumption of fixed certainty is philosophically untenable – Frege's underlying logic is no guarantee of anything – so there is no absolute stable zero point from which uncertainty can be measured. That is why, when I talk about risk management, I do not view translators as calculators, rational egoists, or retainers of some hidden truths – numbers rather than feelings. As I said, the risk is not particularly in the numbers, which means that one is not required to operate in terms of neat calculations of any kind. Risk management is better seen in the use of strategies to avoid communicative failure, to which categories and numbers can sometimes be attached.

That does not mean economics has nothing to say. For example, when I read Kahneman (2011) on psychological experiments where people make decisions in situations of uncertainty, numerous human biases become clear and many of them sound highly applicable to what we find translators doing. At the same time, most of Kahneman's experiments do concern numbers, and the human heuristics are measured in relation to what the rational economic egoist would have done. That is, the economic subject is there, as a reminder that some numbers do win out in the long run, just as the banker always wins whenever I am foolish enough to play blackjack in a casino. You cannot just wish the numbers away.

Anyone who lived through the lockdowns of the COVID pandemic of 2020–21 should be familiar with the language and effects of risk management. Was it ever *just* a question of numbers? For some, the main risk was the loss of life, so we calculated deaths and made people stay at home – numbers on one side (deaths) and numbers on the other (days of lockdown). But lockdowns killed economic and social activity, which was a second kind of risk, so various trade-offs were reached: a certain death rate might be tolerated in the interests of people retaining employment. Numbers against numbers again, as if it were a neutral rationality. Yet the numbers are only responses to the questions asked. When economists argued that risk should be calculated as the probability not of deaths but of years of *productive* life (Foster & Frijters 2022), the greatest negative consequence became the privation of socialization in schools. The risks depend on how the questions are asked, since different questions encapsulate different criteria for success.

The COVID example does have something to do with translation. In Melbourne, where we went through the longest cumulative lockdown in the world, more than 270 languages are spoken at homes, so pandemic information had to be translated. The initial strategy for this was to employ professionally certified translators only, on the supposition that the greatest risk would be the wrong terminology in what looked like medical texts. Other problems soon surfaced, however: professional translations arrived too late to be of use; they were only available in print or on websites, not on the social media where most people were actually going for information; they failed to address and counter conspiracy doxa; they tended not to be trusted in certain language communities; vaccination rates in some language communities were higher than in others (Pym & Hu 2022). The risks were clearly wider and more diverse than mere terminological accuracy. The response was a change in communication strategy, as official messages were relayed to some communities by nonprofessional mediators, particularly trusted people like doctors and religious leaders, who spoke the languages but had no training as translators or interpreters. That was very much a risk-taking change – the government was flouting its own official translation policy, which required the use of certified translators, assuming that they were the ones who could be trusted. Why take that risk? There were numbers to show how aims were *not* being achieved (low vaccination rates, for example), but no numbers to say how they *could* be attained. In this case, the risk-taking generally seemed to pay off, as vaccination rates rose across all language communities, COVID became a memory (for a while), and some official policies have since been modified to include community engagement in addition to professional translation, creating an interesting threat to long-term professionalization processes.

These points have been batting away some of the misconceptions and overstatements that have masqueraded as critiques of the risk-management approach (Gile 2021; Halverson & Kotze 2022; to a lesser extent Robinson 2023). With our sights thus adjusted, we can embark on the more positive and constructive aspects of risk management. The following pages run through the main purposes of translation, the kinds of risk strategy, the importance of trust relations, and the special risks and opportunities of translation automation. If there is one message to be highlighted, it is that translators tend to be risk-averse, keeping their quandaries to themselves, and that more risk-taking is needed if translation is to become a general social activity able to foster long-term cooperation between cultures. However, several steps are needed before that argument can be stated in any full way.

2 Risk of What?

No one does anything just to manage the risks – unless, of course, they are professional risk managers. For the rest of us, there are always aims to achieve, and risk is the probability of not achieving those aims. That means if you want to know about the risks you face, you first have to specify what you are trying to achieve. In this section, I will argue that the general aim of intercultural communication is to achieve cooperation between cultures, so the general risk in this field becomes the probability of noncooperation. The snag is that, just as no one sets out just to manage risks, no one sets out just to cooperate either.

What Is Successful Communication?

When I buy a coffee, I estimate that the pleasure of drinking it is worth more than the effort it would take to make the coffee myself or find an alternative café. And I assume that the price I pay is more than the actual costs paid by the seller – there must be gain for them as well. And even when I am silently puzzled by how anyone can charge so much for a simple cup of coffee (especially in Melbourne), the pleasure is still somehow worth more to me than the effort of finding a cheaper alternative. In fact, the exorbitant price lulls me into assuming the coffee must be exceptionally good, the surroundings astonishingly salubrious, so the risk of bad coffee has been averted and I am supposed to be enjoying the experience. The price might also tell me that the people around me have money and are there for more than a caffeine hit – they might be interesting people with things to say, so I also pay the price for the feeling that I might be one of them. There are many ways to experience value.

Translation is a little like this, although not entirely. If I hire the services of a translator, it is usually because I think the cost will be less than me doing the translation myself. Perhaps I would have to spend years learning a foreign language, which is hardly worthwhile for a one-off message. And even when the translator demands what I think is an exorbitant fee, I might pay it because the high price suggests that the quality is likely to be good, and hopefully good enough to help with my understanding or perhaps my branding or public image – I pay for the assurance of those intangibles. The analogy, however, cannot be pushed too far. In the case of the coffee, I can test part of the quality myself. When it comes to translation, how can I be sure of exactly what I am supposed to be tasting? Something might be askew or missing – there might be a great translation somewhere, possibly here in front of me, but if the original language is foreign to me, how could I be sure? And if the translation is going *into* a foreign context, how could I ever get the feeling that it is entirely appropriate, fitting in with the right people? Communicative success cannot really be tested there. There is simply a lot more uncertainty.

Is There Ever Just One Purpose?

Let us try another approach. A whole school of translation theory asserts that a translation should be judged successful when it achieves its purpose (for which they use the German-Greek term *Skopos*). That means that if the purpose of a translated publicity campaign is to sell cars, the pertinent risk will be that not many cars are sold. Or if the aim of vaccination information is for people to get vaccinated, the risk will be that they do not trust the information and do not get vaccinated. That much is clear and incontrovertible. In those cases, a certain success can be expressed in numbers and a mathematical kind of risk can be calculated.

A problem with that theory is that we very rarely act to achieve just one aim, just as there is never only one reason for paying too much for a cup of coffee. Think, for a moment, about the reasons why you are reading this page, and the reasons why you might be thinking of not progressing to the next one. To make more money as a translator? To prepare for an exam? To argue about concepts of risk? To satisfy curiosity? To escape boredom? To get to sleep? Any number of purposes are involved, and I am probably failing to help you attain most of them. Perhaps more worrying, I do not really have just one purpose in *writing* these lines, and the aims that I do have are very likely not to meet up neatly with yours. The simple linear correspondence presupposed by *Skopos* theory (success from just one agreed purpose) is rarely in evidence.

Should we perhaps accept that the pertinent aim is whatever the translator says it is? Here is a translator telling us why he chose to render a novel in a certain way:

> The aim was to immerse the reader in a world that is noticeably distant in time, but nonetheless affecting in contemporary terms – to compel a participation in the emotional extravagance that drives this wildly romantic novel, but without losing the awareness that the prose is over the top. (Venuti 1994: xi)

That aim is certainly not simple: a narrative world that is both distant and contemporary, seeking "participation" in something that is at the same time "over the top." This is very paradoxical and ambitious. What were the risks involved? How many readers could actually follow those instructions and experience all those things?

In this case, the translator was also a translation scholar who was strangely happy to tell us what happened. A reviewer at the *New York Review of Books* noticed the intended exaggeration but could not follow it. Faced with a phrase like "the funk wherein I fell" (Tarchetti 1994: 125), how is one to make the archaic syntax accord with the twentieth-century American slang? The reviewer can only ask, "Is this guy for real?" (Harrison 1994: 8). The reviewer did not appreciate the translation. The translator consequently complained that the reviewer had "refused to understand it according to the explanation presented in my introduction" (Venuti 1998: 19). That is, the reviewer had sought purposes other than the ones that the translator had told her she should enact. One kind of complex purpose might have been crystal-clear to the translator, but it was *not* shared by the receiver. The outcome was, in the eyes of both the translator and the reviewer, a moment of communicative failure. One person was looking for one thing, the other person was looking for something else. It is not enough to have a purpose and then insist that everyone else should share it – you cannot tell your communication partners how they must interpret you. Communication requires more than that.

What Is Cooperation?

Let us try yet another approach. The success of communication can also be indicated by the participants' shared desire to keep communicating. When viewers abandon a film or a reader loses interest in a character ("Is this guy for real?"), something has gone wrong. And when, on the other hand, the people agree to keep communicating, something is going right: the book reviewer will encourage more translations of a certain kind, and the translator will keep producing translations, perhaps working the edges of the reviewer's expectations and moving them toward new experiences. That kind of success is much more diffuse and variable than the simple achievement of a clear purpose. It can help us propose something like a general aim for communication, and thereby for translations.

When people agree to keep communicating, they usually do so because they hope they can gain something from the activity. More precisely, the hope should be that there is more to gain from communicating with a particular person or group than from *not* communicating with them or from communicating with someone else. When two or more participants all hope to gain more from the communication than from the alternatives, then the communication can be said to be successful. More technically, we can say that there is a shared expectation of mutual benefits (everyone gains something), which is another name for cooperation. Risk, in the most general case, is then the probability of noncooperation – which becomes another name for failed communication.

That little piece of theorizing has something magical in it. It basically says that if communication is a game, then it is not of the kind where if I win, you lose (a zero-sum game). It is a game where all participants can win more than they started with, although the gains have no need to be equal. There are capitalist theories that tie this idea to Adam Smith's observation that competition between international traders can produce social gains (1776/2000: 4.2). But there are just as many theories that see cooperation as the basis of human social organization, and language as developing to coordinate cooperative activities of all kinds: "Social cooperation is our key for survival and reproduction" (Harari 2014: 27). When I propose that long-term cooperation is a general goal for cross-cultural communication, the underlying assumption is that it is good for different cultures to cooperate with each other because there are mutual benefits to be sought.

That idea is not well understood. Cooperation is not just about everyone getting on well together, like cute tales of rabbits and butterflies. The theory only requires that each participant can hope to gain more from the interaction than they put in – the result is win-win, not everyone winning the *same* amount. Importantly, this view of cooperation does *not* assume that the participants are equal – cooperation can operate in highly asymmetric situations, often with marked power differentials. And it does not assume that anyone is calculating the gains in any exact way, not any more than the value of my cup of coffee is an exact calculation. We engage in cooperation on the basis of rough estimations and trial-and-error, with losses and gains that are as much psychological as they could be financial.

How Can Anyone Measure Success or Failure in Communication?

In terms of cooperation, failure is noncooperation, the most extreme form of which is betrayal. As is suggested by the Italian adage *traduttore, traditore* ('translator, traitor'), translation is always tinged with the possibility of treason. To appreciate this, you really have to be in a negotiation where you do not know the language of the other side and you therefore depend on a mediator of some kind. How can you trust the mediator is not operating in the interests of the other side? After all, the person in the middle speaks the language of the other side and knows their culture. And perhaps you are not paying them enough?

That particular uncertainty – the risk of betrayal – is curiously foundational for translation. It makes *credibility* the translator's prime stock in trade, to the extent that the translator's greatest personal risk is the loss of perceived trustworthiness.

For all their intellectual and ethical virtues, the concepts of cooperation and betrayal remain abstract. Worse, they are not strictly necessary for any of the other concepts involved in risk management. One could reject the role of cooperation as a noble, unifying aim and still apply risk management to any other general or specific purpose. One could regard betrayal as an improbable one-off event that is without consequence for general work on translation – incompetence is a more prevalent risk. Indeed, it is important to accept that, in each communicative situation, there are many particular aims involved and their identification is not a mechanical process. Each participant has an idea of the kinds of gains they are seeking, and there is no reason why those aims should all be the same. So how can anyone possibly judge whether the communication is successful?

What other kinds of aims are pertinent to risk in a communication act? When looking at an exchange from the outside, it is often quite hard to tell. One way to approach pertinent aims is to ask not what the ideal outcome will be for all concerned (individual partners may at best have a vague idea), but *what are the worst things that can happen*? What is the greatest hazard that each participant wants to avoid? The answers to that question can point to where the risks are and where some risk management is needed. More importantly, that kind of negative question helps us avoid empty and unattainable ideals of perfect understanding in a perfect communication situation.

An example I use to illustrate this in class is a 2008 television report on an interpreter working for the United States military in Afghanistan (Pym 2016).

Missiles have been coming at the Americans from the vicinity of a village, so a patrol goes to inspect. It is a complex interaction involving the village (although almost everyone has fled), the patrol sergeant, an old man speaking on behalf of the village (explaining why they have left), and an Afghan interpreter. For each of these actors, it is possible to project the worst communication outcomes and thereby hypothesize explanations for their risk management. The sergeant does not want more bombs, so the very presence of the patrol is supposed to tell the village not to accept the Taliban – but the presence sends this message anyway, so not much translating is needed there. The village knows it has nothing to gain from interaction with the Americans, so they have all left – no translating needed there. Like an abandoned lover, the sergeant is left with no mutual benefits to offer and no one to have a conversation with. Eventually, the old man comes along and has a story to narrate. He tells a parable about ants eating wheat, which in context is understandable as saying but not saying that the Taliban will always be there and have to be tolerated, whereas the Americans will be leaving. He tells the story in Pashto, so translation is needed. What is the Afghan interpreter's risk management? His worst outcome would be to stay in the country when the Taliban come to power, so he has absolutely nothing to gain from relating the old man's parable. His strategy is instead to tell his employers exactly what they want to hear: "He is giving many examples, sir. But the bombs are coming from behind that hill . . . . I ask them questions, they give the wrong answers." That is not exactly in the playbook of best practices for interpreters. The interpreter's subterfuge nevertheless makes perfect sense in terms of risk management, and it worked in the context of the immediate exchanges. In fact, it might have worked long-term were it not for the presence of a television camera and the subsequent appearance of some subtitles on the video report. The strange thing about this complex interaction is that no one achieves an entirely positive outcome, and yet everyone avoids their worst options. The theory of cooperation allows us to see that possibility – it can help make sense of an interpreted encounter that otherwise would be merely reprehensible in any professional terms.

We have done similar analyses on other kinds of nonstandard practices. In the Barcelona courts, recordings show interpreters having one-on-one conversations with defendants (Pym, Raigal-Aran, & Bestué Salinas 2023). The practice goes against all professional guidelines, but it usually enables the judge to ensure that a plea deal has been understood and thus efficiently helps all participants avoid their worst outcomes.

Analysis of these kinds of examples suggests that there may be a general principle involved. If we ask what might be the worst possible outcome of a translated exchange, one can often point to *the relative proximity of alternative nonlinguistic action*, sometimes violent: the bombs fall, the interpreter is killed as a traitor, the defendant is unjustly imprisoned or, more probably, is deported following a plea deal that is not understood. One communicates to avoid bad things. And the special importance of spoken interactions, with interpreters, may lie in the greater spatial and temporal proximity of those bad things.

Who Cooperates?

When there is a communication situation like an army patrol or a courtroom, cooperation can first be sought between those present in the scene. They usually have asymmetric power relations but can still enter into cooperation: it is enough that each participant improves their starting point; once again, mutual benefits have no need to be equal.

There are, of course, many other people and factors that might be affected in some way and that probably reap much slimmer benefits or are harmed. Cooperation could also concern the long-term fate of Afghan society, justice for immigrant groups, the North-South divide, the prolonged viability of the translation profession, the environmental consequences of translation technologies, and so on. In theory, cooperation can be sought on any level of interaction, and the imperatives of ethical critique should push us toward those wider, more general considerations.

The kind of risk management I am interested in here nevertheless starts from the local decision-making process, between the people and factors considered pertinent by the decision maker. When Eugen Dollmann interpreted between Hitler and Mussolini (entertainingly recounted in Dollmann 1967), one should ethically regret that his risk assessments did not extend more widely beyond seeking cooperation between the two leaders, but we must accept that his decision-making first concerned the people and factors present in his historical scene. We must try to understand why risk was managed in certain ways through those local decisions, and only then move on to the wider ethical critiques. If not, we simply impose our own priorities.

Failure Can Be Economic

The theory of mutual benefits allows a certain economic approach to communicative failure. The rule of thumb is that *the effort each person puts into the interaction should be worth less to them than the value of what they gain*. This is a basic principle of appropriate transaction costs that I played with some years ago (Pym 1995). For example, the Barcelona judge could require, in accordance with the code of ethics, that interpreters never speak in their own voice and that they render everything into the language of the court, but the effort would be much greater than the side conversations that the judge allows to happen in untranslated English between the interpreter and the defendant. The actual gains of applying standard practice would be minimal: the judge would have to trust the interpreter's intervention anyway. In such situations – and there are many – cheap communication can be justified, and so can cheap translation. In technical terms, one need only insist that, for each participant, the transaction costs (the sum of the efforts put into the communication) must be less than the perceived benefits of the communication.

That abstract theory sometimes assumes an economic rationalist who can compare the values of initially incommensurate items: effort, benefits, and risk in terms of the magnitude and predicted frequency of failure. Yes, one might like to imagine there is a small economist in us calculating those things. But, again, the process is no more complex, calculated, or exact than the experience of paying for a coffee. When I stop watching a film, I judge that the effort I am investing is worth more than the pleasure I am receiving. I might take a risk and decide to try for a few minutes more, in the hope that my effort will be reduced or the pleasure increased. But the experience is psychological, not particularly economic.

In some translation situations, the transaction costs are higher than might be considered appropriate and the economic costs are indeed pertinent. Many years ago, I worked externally on European Commission documents that needed to be translated to satisfy the official language policy and for no other reason. For example, a meeting had been held in English but the minutes had to be translated nonetheless. No one was ever going to read the translated minutes. My work effectively created what Koskinen (2008) terms 'existential translations,' since all they have to do is exist. The one translation instruction was to avoid contradictions. Similarly, long documents are too often fully translated by highly qualified humans at considerable cost just to see if there are a few pages that need to be understood, whereas a quick summary or gist translation could have helped locate the few pages that warrant a translator's full attention. This is where machine translation has long had a role to play (Church & Hovy 1993). And translators can and should be trained in the skills of locating what really has to be translated (Gouadec 2007).

The idea that cheap communication can be good communication is by no means music to the ears of all the good translation professionals who are struggling to be paid what they are worth. The principle can nevertheless help us understand why automated translation (machine translation and generative AI) has found a vital and truly useful role in the world, and why professional translations are best kept for high-stakes situations where there is something important to win or lose. The financial problems may not ensue from the technologies alone, but from the false assumptions that risks are the same in all communication acts and that professional translation is somehow the only way to communicate across languages.

The rationalist economic theory on this point is not entirely banal. When transaction costs are low, more people can communicate in interactions, which is itself a democratic virtue. And the more people can participate, the more possible it becomes for you to find the most suitable partner for your specific interactions (the best film for you to watch, the most important pages to translate, the best trading partner for your goods or services, the best future spouse). The one snag, for economic theory, is that the greater the number of people entering into an exchange, the harder it becomes to locate the most appropriate partners. From that perspective, the possibilities for cooperation are enhanced by people who discount themselves or otherwise withdraw from the communicative situation: your potential lover says they do not want to see you anymore, so you are free to turn your efforts elsewhere; a declaration of war tells the other party that there no need to invest more effort in peace negotiations. Those kinds of negative acts have positive virtues from the perspective of cooperation theory.

More provocatively, that particular theory of cooperation suggests that high numbers of translations can be a bad thing. When we try to translate everything, in all directions, it is hard to find what is worth translating in the interests of mutual benefits.

Why Is Intercultural Communication Especially Prone to Risk?

Risk management is only required in situations of uncertainty when there are doubts about the cooperative outcomes of present actions. I suspect that communication between cultures, particularly when different languages are involved, involves fewer shared communication patterns than communication within a culture. This gives rise to greater uncertainty about the intentions and expectations of the communication partner, who could potentially betray you. That greater uncertainty means that the risks of noncooperation become greater, as does the need for specific kinds of risk management. That is pure theory, of course, but it can help explain why translators are important and why they should be paid well. The greater the uncertainty, the greater the efforts needed to reduce it, and the more value that reduction of uncertainty will have.

As noted, one problem with that theory is the way it assumes there is a place where absolute certainty prevails, presumably somewhere near the center of a culture: in the routines of the family breakfast, the innuendos of jokes shared with old friends, in the complete trust of the babe in arms, perhaps in the womb?

When the deconstructionist Rosemary Arrojo debated translation with the more analytical thinker Andrew Chesterman (Chesterman & Arrojo 2000), this was the one major point that she refused to accept: that there are points of greater or lesser certainty. To accept that idea, she would have had to accept that there was a point of absolute certainty from which uncertainty could be measured. For deconstruction, there is no such point.

I think Arrojo was too puristic in her stance. It is enough to recognize that the complexities of uncertainty are reduced by power (the authorities that seek to control language), routine (the familiarity that enables implicitness), and trust (the active decision to suspend doubts), and none of those factors need eradicate uncertainty entirely. There is no overwhelming requirement for those social and psychological processes to reach a zero point – one can challenge power, change routine, and temper trust – and no reason to limit uncertainty to the appearance of something new – deep doubts can nestle in the most habitual of daily actions, as when we know members of our family so well that we choose not to trust them. Yet the forces and practices by which uncertainty is reduced must be recognized as parts of social life, even when we do not want them to be, or we are not conscious of them. Visiting the poorly known land of my father's family, I was identified from a distance: "You walk like your grandfather."

Why Look at Translation in These Terms?

Are there points of relatively high certainty? Of course there are when it is a question of obeying the authorities of grammar and terminology, or when accrued experience guides you. Do such points need translating? They certainly concern things that translators do, but one could choose to keep a strong sense of 'translation' for problems where the choices are not made by reference to authoritative rules or precedent and where some kind of more interesting risk management is required.

As I have indicated, if translation is thought of in a rule-bound way, in terms of fidelity or equivalence, the only risk would be of misrepresenting an anterior text. On the other hand, when translators are seen as choosing between more or less viable alternatives, when you appreciate that they are actively interpreting language and projecting reception effects, adjusting to new receivers and new situations, there are no clear-cut rules for reducing the uncertainty. The resulting variability can be hidden when someone simply believes that the translation is 'equivalent.' But once you are aware of the uncertainty, and hence of the alternatives, then some more complex and engaging kind of risk management is required.

3 Types of Risk Management

This section explains the major classical risk strategies and how they can help explain translators' decisions. Awareness of this range can also hopefully broaden the vision of anyone faced with making risk-management decisions, especially novices.

Adjust Effort to What Is at Stake

Let us suppose that some parts of a text involve higher stakes than others, in the sense that they are more important for fostering cooperation. It would make sound economic sense for a translator to work hardest on those higher-stakes parts, and less on the parts that are less important. That applies something like a law of least effort, but it could also be simple common sense. I once presented this idea to a hundred or so translation consultants at the World Bible Society – people who enthusiastically translate monotheism into the languages of jungles and deserts. A group of them reported back from their workshop that, in their handfuls of local vernaculars, it was not hard to find errors and infelicities in the least-read parts of the Bible, particularly something like Chronicles ("And Joktan begat Almodad, and Sheleph, and Hazarmaveth, and Jerah," etc.). Do those names matter to anyone? Why spend time on their translation?

This most basic of risk-management strategies is perhaps the hardest to learn and apply. Novice translators tend to invest too much effort in low-stakes problems (producing overwork and missed deadlines) or too little effort in high-stakes problems (leading to high-risk guessing games) (Pym 1995). A little training in the basics of risk management can help them avoid those two extremes – without converting them into rational egoists.

An unfortunately traditional attitude in translator training is nevertheless to insist that everything in the text is important, such that errors are penalized equally no matter where and when they occur. There are reasons for this (as I will discuss when considering the importance of trust), but the professional quality metrics do usually weight major and minor errors differently. If there is no such weighting, the effect is to make the translator pay the utmost attention to everything, thereby increasing the human effort put into translations and helping to make translation an even more luxurious communication option. As I have argued earlier, unreasonably high transaction costs can have negative social effects on cross-cultural communication.

Automated translations (machine translation or generative AI) offer many ways of reducing transaction costs. However, they currently cannot effectively adjust efforts to variable risks in the way that humans can (Pym 2020: 454). In our work on the use of machine translation in emergency messaging (Hajek et al. 2024), the errors of human translators or posteditors were very rarely in the high-stakes parts of texts, while those of automation could be anywhere. That is one of the major advantages of being human: we can sense danger and avoid it, sometimes excessively.

When and How to Avoid Risks

Risk avoidance occurs when points of uncertainty are avoided or reduced, often through omission or the reduction of specificity. Translators tend to play it safe. In terms of personalities, they may be risk-averse.

There are numerous ways in which risks are avoided. Some of the best evidence of avoidance comes from studies that identify the ways the language in translations tends to differ from that of non-translations (either start texts or parallel texts[1]). Levý (1963/2011) called these 'translation tendencies,' although they are also known as 'universals' (Pym 2023a: 93–99). For example, translations tend to have less lexical variation (Blum-Kulka & Levenston 1983; Vanderauwera 1985; Toury 2012: 303–306), making the language flatter and potentially more boring than original texts. Why should this happen? It could be that translators do not want to use low-frequency words whose meanings are not widely understood. They would thus be trying to avoid misunderstanding. Of course, the reasons might also be that the translator is not paid enough to find a lot of different words, is under too much time pressure, is uncertain about what words are less frequent in the target-text genre, or does not know anything specific about who the receiver is or what the text is for. These are all possible reasons for the linguistic observation – we cannot say for sure that there has been any specific attempt to manage risk by limiting the range of words. But we can suggest that the effect of these reasons is to create a flatter, more boring text, with which less can go wrong in the receptions downstream. To ascertain anything like an actual cause, we would need more evidence than text comparison can provide, but the general tendency is nevertheless compatible with a strategy of avoiding risks in the space of reception, in fact with making things easier for the receiver.

The other tendencies can be interpreted in much the same way. When we are told that translations tend to have more cohesion devices (Blum-Kulka 1986), words that are more general in meaning (Klaudy 1993), clearer punctuation (Malmkjær 1997), and fewer incomplete sentences or otherwise nonstandard structures (Vanderauwera 1985), it seems that the text is being made easier for the new receiver to work with, possibly because there is uncertainty about what

---

[1] The term 'start text' is used here instead of the more traditional 'source text' because translators these days work from clients' instructions, translation memories, glossaries, machine translation, and generative AI proposals, all of which are also 'sources.' A 'parallel text' is a text in the target language that is on the same topic as the start text.

routines or accrued familiarity can be shared with that reader. Similarly, when Shlesinger (1989) finds that interpreters tend to tone down language that is highly colloquial or highly formal, avoiding the two extremes of register, they would seem to be playing it safe (Pym 2007). I might also add that, in some genres, interpreters' renditions commonly make use of omissions (Pym 2008), which can also make a text easier to understand, even when it is a strategy that few professionals want to admit to.

With respect to all those features, cooperation theory can provide something like a plausible account. The text has traveled away from its place of production; the shared routines, familiarity, and trust relations have diminished; uncertainty has thus grown; the translator therefore compensates for the uncertainty by offering the reader fewer linguistic challenges and more communicative clues (cf. Malmkjær 2005). This reduces the cognitive efforts required and thereby widens the catchment of possible cooperation partners. Of course, once again, it might also be that the translator is underpaid, short of time, and/or unadventurous by nature, which would all be reasons for avoiding risks. As I say, we need more than the text to ascertain anything like a cause.

Another case of risk aversion might be the translation of swearing. It is generally found that translations tone down or omit taboo words (see the studies summarized in Hjort 2017). This is possibly because the words are felt to be stronger in one's first language (as suggested by Hjort), although one might equally suppose that a translator working into their second language plays it safe because of the greater uncertainty of the semantic charges involved. Whatever the direction, translators tend not to swear as much as non-translators. Interestingly, Samir (2024) reports that Iranian women translators tend to tone down taboo words more than Iranian men translators do, indicating that this part of risk management may be gendered.

Textual comparisons provide a few further phenomena that are a little more difficult to interpret in terms of cooperation. Vandevoorde and Lefever (2023) report evidence for what they term the 'fear of false friends hypothesis': the higher the level of cognateness between two languages, the more translators will be hesitant to use cognate translations (words that have similar origins but different meanings). For instance, the English *brave* looks like the Dutch *braaf*, but the meanings of the latter also cover the semantic territory of 'good' or 'well-behaved.' In some cases, translators could use the Dutch to translate the English, but the risk of a non-corresponding meaning is presumably so ingrained in their habitus that they tend to avoid the cognates, preferring something visibly different like *moedig* (brave). This risk-averse behavior means that there tend to be fewer cognates in translations than in non-translations, which is another reason why the language in translations can sound flatter. The excessive caution probably has as much to do with the fear of error as with the idea of cooperating with a receiver. Its effects are to make the translator's work a little harder and the resulting translations, once again, a little more boring.

A more complex problem concerns lexical 'explicitation,' understood as a translation solution where something that is implicit in the start text is spelled out in the translation. A classic example is the name *Eton* in an English text, which could become something like "the exclusive private school Eton" when translated outside the United Kingdom (Hönig & Kussmaul 1982: 53). This makes sense and can even be seen as an indication of a good translator at work, helping the reader understand the foreign culture. But is this truly risk avoidance? The problem with lexical explicitation is that the translator must be *very sure* that the explicated content was indeed implicit, since the information is not obvious in the start text, by definition. In the case of Eton, how can the translator really know that 'exclusive' and 'private' are the *only* semantic values that come to an English reader of the text? The translator can hazard a good guess, but that implies *taking* a risk, not avoiding risks. More problematic are the not infrequent cases of expert-to-expert communication, where the participants in the communication have different languages but they all know the field of knowledge better than the translator or interpreter (Shlesinger 1989; Pym 2007). In such cases, any explicitation becomes an act of risk-taking, and 'playing it safe' means opting for implicitation instead. In my occasional adventures as a simultaneous interpreter at medical conferences, one of my favorite go-to strategies in moments of doubt was 'As you can see on the screen . . . .' The presentation slides had all the information; the participants knew what was going on; I had no reason to make guesses and much less reason to risk anything like an explicitation. I suspect it is for this basic reason that theorists like Gutt (1991) and Vázquez-Ayora (1977: 288) view elaborate explicitations as lying beyond the responsibility of the translator – the risks can be too great. In the context of risk management, explicitation may look like risk aversion but it is better analyzed in terms of trade-offs, as we shall see later.

When and How to Transfer Risks

Risk transfer occurs when the translator reduces uncertainty by passing responsibility for possible failure onto someone else. This may involve consulting the client, referring to an authoritative source, or adopting certain modes of literalism. Most of these strategies move risk *upstream*, away from the translator and away from the end users.

The French translator trainer Daniel Gouadec (2007) has various models of the translation process in which almost all the steps involve checking the start text, locating or producing glossaries, identifying reliable parallel texts, and selecting a style sheet. Then there is a small intermediate step called 'translation,' which is followed by a complicated quality-control and postmortem process. The basic message is that extensive preparation can reduce uncertainty to a very low level, which means that the actual translation process is relatively straightforward. (It never is, in my experience, but let's go with Gouadec's model.) What is of most interest is that, at the end of the extensive preparations, the translator or project manager is advised to prepare a short list of 'options,' basically questions that remain unresolved: whether to use the formal or informal second person, which variety of the target language to work into (British or American English, for example), how to interpret key terms, and so on. Those questions are then presented to the client, who says how they should be resolved. Does that mean the client is an expert in such matters? Often not. But if *they* make those decisions, then the translator can never be responsible for the consequences. The risk of error in those matters has effectively been transferred to the client.

This kind of transfer can happen rather less systematically. Matsushita (2016: 156; cf. Pym & Matsushita 2018) reports the case of a consecutive interpreter working at a press conference given in 2013 by the Mayor of Osaka. When he came to the delicate issue of Japan's wartime involvement and the forced use of women as sexual slaves for their army:

> ST4: ただ、この慰安婦問題に関して、不合理な議論はもう終止符を打つべきだと思っています
>
> [However, I think that we should put an end to such fugori debate regarding this comfort women issue.]
>
> Interpreter: Having said all of this, however, I believe that we have now reached a point in time where we should perhaps put an end to what I would call ... *fugori* is the word that the mayor is using ... perhaps irrational, or unreasonable arguments or debates.

Here the risk management is similar, except that the use of the Japanese term introduces a change of footing: the interpreter refers to the speaker in the third person, thereby assuming a first-person discourse for herself (technically breaking with her translational use of the alien-I).

Another way of transferring risk is through astute implicitation. I remember stumbling across this back in the pre-Internet days when information was hard to come by and so was money – I had to translate fast. I was translating a letter addressed to the 'Asociación Internacional de Colombofilia' (recounted in Pym 1993), which could be rendered as the 'International Pigeon Association,' 'International Pigeon-Fanciers Association,' 'International Colombophile Association,' or several more. How was I to know? No way of asking the client, since the work came from an agency. So I rendered the text as addressing 'the members of the association,' since those members would presumably know what their association was called. Problem solved – the risk was transferred downstream, to the place of the reader. (Now, with Internet access, the problem is solved in a second: the association is called the FCI, for the French 'Fédération Colombophile Internationale.')

A more widespread way of transferring risk involves certain forms of literalism, in the sense of sticking closely to the forms of the start text and making only the adjustments that are linguistically necessary. This is in some ways the opposite of the risk-avoidance tendencies that we have just seen, since the effect can be to make the translation relatively *difficult* for the new receiver: the translation will bear traces of interference from the start language and text. Translations of company chairpersons' statements, for example, have been found to "frequently retain the formality of the original documents [and] may also appear less engaging or personalized than their native counterparts" (Wang & Liu 2024: 14). Why should that happen? Translators at the European Commission are similarly reported as paying special attention to legal acts and quotations when doing postediting, always checking with the original text in such cases (Lesznyák 2019). Why do this? When investor confidence and legal implications are at stake and you have little to gain personally, you do not want to gamble. But neither can you simply spirit the risks away through simplification, generalization, or omission. And when you are additionally dealing with the boss's words, you know the boss probably wants to recognize their own voice – they may well be your first and most important reader. These, I propose, are all reasons for risk transfer through literalism. In the event that there are misunderstandings downstream, any blame for the strange-sounding text might come back to the translator, but the translator can then always point back to the syntactic formulation of the law or particular style of the author. Don't blame the messenger!

Bei Hu (2020) reports something similar happening with translators of foreign-affairs texts in China. The translators are not particularly aware of addressing any readers outside of China, but they are very conscious of their supervisors as their first and most powerful readers. Perhaps in the same vein, novice translators at the United Nations are revised by a superior for their first two years (Lafeber 2022), making the superior the first and most important reader of the translations. The psychological effect in both cases is to hide the image of an external receiver. The result, however, is not necessarily recourse to literalism. In both these cases, translators learn to write in the house style and, in the Chinese case, to adopt the established terms and phrases of the foreign-discourse system. The style sheets, writing guides, and glossaries (and increasingly translation memories) not only provide a safe harbor amid uncertainty, but they effectively enable the translator to transfer the risk of error or misunderstanding. 'Don't blame me! I just applied the rules!' In these cases, risk is not just avoided, it is sent upstream.

A parallel case would be official audiovisual translations on Catalan public television, where the translators are obliged to follow the official style guide both for the subtitles and for the kind of Catalan they use. The political purpose of the television channels is to defend and extend the Catalan language. So while the surrounding society uses extensive code-switching between Catalan and Spanish, that almost never happens in the official media. Risk is transferred to the institution.

Of course, a literalist strategy might also involve an effort-saving dimension as well. When I translated the speeches of the President of Catalonia into English, many years ago, I struggled with his roundabout syntax and non-sequential logic; I tried to make everything as clear and as linear as possible for the English-language reader. If not, how could anyone follow? Why would they ever vote for this guy? After a few speeches, I was told that the president had not appreciated my efforts (everyone reads English or thinks they can). I then adopted literalism, not just in the interests of expediency but also, I told myself, in the name of democracy: if someone was going to vote for this person, they had every right to see how his mind worked, not how logical his translator was. One speech, presenting his candidacy to be elected Chair of the European Council of Regions, was particularly spaghetti-like in Catalan. I gave it the same qualities in English, closing my eyes and playing it safe. He was elected.

One of the examples I use to illustrate risk transfer is from the 1970 film *Patton*. Immediately after the fall of Nazi Berlin, the American general George Patton confronts the Soviet general Gregori Zhukov at an American-Soviet celebration. There is no communication between the two generals (no mutual benefits to be sought) until the Soviet proposes a toast to the surrender of Germany. Patton instructs his interpreter (reportedly Colonel Edgar Zaharia), with a smile: "Please inform the general I do not care to drink with him, or any other Russian son of a bitch." The interpreter understandably doubts this is likely to improve international cooperation: "Sir, I can't tell the general that … ." The general insists: "Tell him word for word." the interpreter interprets, and the Soviet's relayed reply comes back as "The general says he thinks you are a son of a bitch too." And then there is a toast.

The interpreter was undoubtedly correct to warn the general of the risks involved: World War Three could have started immediately in Berlin. He was also astute in changing the footing when reporting the Russian: "The general says … " breaks with the alien-I and removes his own position from the utterance, transferring some risk in the direction of the Russian. But he was also correct in ultimately allowing the American general to choose his own discursive path. In having it known that there was no cooperation to be sought, the two generals understood each other and allowed each other to seek cooperative relations in their separate parts of the world. The Cold War began. Politicians, CEOs, and generals are paid to take such risks. Translators mostly are not.

When and How to Take Risks

Risk-taking involves accepting a certain probability of communicative failure and proceeding regardless. Although the evidence from textual comparison suggests that translators tend to be risk-averse, there are several reasons why they might decide to take risks.

One of them, best dismissed quickly, is stupidity. For example, a student looks for a matching term in a bilingual dictionary; there are three possible terms; two of them are recognized and do not sound appropriate; so the student opts for the third term, the unknown one, applying a process of elimination. Sometimes they might be right, but language usually does not work that way. Better to keep looking or use some risk avoidance or risk transfer.

Speed is perhaps the major motivation for calculated risk-taking. Every year the Nobel Prize in Literature is announced in October, and then publishers in much of the Western world attempt to get the winner translated and published for the Christmas market. Hansson (2022) recounts how she translated a novel by the 2021 winner Abdulrazak Gurnah in some five weeks, by herself, when the task would normally have taken at least twice that long – this was "translation as an extreme sport," as she put it. Other examples are best-sellers where there is competition in the market. For Dan Brown's *The Da Vinci Code* – not a Nobel Prize winner by any means, but an international best-seller – the bookshops in Barcelona could sell translations in Catalan or Spanish, and whichever version arrived first would sell more copies. Legend has it that the Catalan version was done by two translators, who took one half each, so the female protagonist in the novel was called 'Sophie' in one half and 'Sofia' in the other – which is actually not the case in the copy I have. But there is a dissertation that notes fifty errors in the Spanish version (Senmache Artola 2019), and a small discussion thread lamenting errors in the Catalan (Racó català 2004). In all these cases, the added risks incurred by speed are offset by the lure of commercial sales.

One would like to say that these cases of speed-induced risk-taking are merely anecdotal. In much of the translation industry, though, the project deadline is more important than any ideal of high translation quality, so it is logical to accept certain risks in the translation process. Sometimes this can reach slightly perverse extremes. I was once applying for a research project in Spain on the uses of machine translation. The application documents asked for letters from industry partners affirming the importance of the project and the transferability of the results. I asked for letters from various companies, received some great supportive documents in English, and submitted the application on time. Three months later, I received the supportive letter I had requested from the Directorate General for Translation at the European Commission – in very beautiful Spanish, since I was in Spain when I asked for it and language policy somewhere said that they should communicate with me in that language. Great letter, but too late to be of any use! (By the way, I did not get the grant. One of the evaluators said that with so much support from industry, why would I need public funding?)

There is a more internal kind of risk-taking involved when a translator is not sure how a rendition will be received but selects it anyway, perhaps as an experiment. This sometimes takes us back to stupidity. When I was a youthful, enthusiastic translator – back in the days of typewriters – I rendered a few chapters of a friend's novel from Spanish into English, except that I chose to go into Australian English. There was nothing in the novel that particularly justified the use of Australian colloquialisms. I was simply wondering why translations somehow had to go systematically into one of the major varieties of English and never into a more minor variety. When I showed those chapters to a few Australian friends, they quickly made me realize the experiment was not going to work. There was no reason why Spanish characters should be speaking Australian English (like Venuti's nineteenth-century Italian getting into a 'funk') – no one was going to take it seriously. I returned to standard English. The risk here was admittedly not great, and the cost could be measured in a few hours. But a risk had been taken.

That experience came back to haunt me some years later when I translated a film script from Spanish into English for the director Bigas Luna (now sadly passed away, so I can tell the tale). Since one of the characters was markedly Italian, I gave him markedly Italian English, just out of fun. I should have known better: any accents enter the scene much later in the production phase. So again, I lost a few hours on a linguistic folly. This time, though, I was not paid for the translation, and I still have not been paid. The producer that was supposed to pay me is a company called Rodeo Drive, perhaps a cowboy outfit, located in Rome. They probably thought I was making fun of Italians, and so I accepted the negative consequences of my risk-taking. For the record, there are quite a few publishers who still owe me for translations, especially Edicions del Serbal in Barcelona and Ediciones Oroel in Zaragoza. In those cases, I was probably taking a few more risks than I was aware of, basically by not checking the reliability of my communication partners – but that is Business 101, not particularly specific to translation.

A more intimate kind of risk-taking involves making translation choices that are designed to attract attention despite significant underlying doubt. An example analyzed by Qiu (2024) is the Chinese expression 江湖 (*jianghu*), which translates literally as 'lakes and rivers.' The term is used in classical Chinese literature to refer to a rural world where bandits roam and superhuman fights take place. In English translations of the narratives, it is commonly omitted (risk aversion) or translated literally (risk-taking, presumably unsuccessful). Neither strategy is going to help the reader very much. In fansubs of audiovisual versions, however, the established translation has become *the Pugilist world*, which for many receivers probably makes as little sense as the literal *lakes and rivers*. If the receiver knows that *pugilist* refers to boxing (from the Latin *pugnus* for fist), then they might stand a chance of relating the expression to martial arts. If not, no matter: it seems that repetition of *the Pugilist world* in context after context has made the reference clear enough for the repetitions to continue. A major risk was taken by some anonymous translator, and the result has been the general acceptance of a new term. The risk paid off.

Similar examples concern successful guesses or uninformed 'flying blind' literalism. A favorite example of mine comes from medieval translations of medical texts from Arabic into Latin (Pym 2014: 37). One of the causes of skin infections in the Latin of Girardus and Alpagus is a *planta noctis* (night plant) (Sudhoff 1909), where the 'plant' part entered history as a translation of the Arabic نبات (*nabat*, plant). For several centuries, Western medicine had to watch out for this mysterious plant of the night. Later, when Spanish conquistadores brought back 'new' diseases from the Americas, Western medical scholars realized that the Arabic *nabat* should have been *banat* (بنات), distinguished only by misplaced or more probably absent diacritics (نبات vs. بنات). The reference was to 'daughters of the night,' prostitutes, and the skin infection was syphilis. The twelfth-century translators had no idea what the text referred to, so they used literalism as a wild guess – let someone down the line sort it out! And when the knowledge was needed, it was there to be recuperated.

You might argue that this literalism is a case of risk avoidance, passing the risk upstream to the defective start text. In this case, however, there seems to be little sense of playing it safe – the translators had no way of estimating the risks to be avoided, so they were condemned to take risks. Alternatively, one might want to see this as risk transfer, since the problem is effectively sent downstream for resolution. However, it is difficult to imagine how the translators thereby avoided responsibility for the erroneous 'night plant.' They were taking a risk, and one supposes they knew they were taking it.

To venture a generalization, risk-taking strategies mostly move risk *downstream*, away from the translator and toward the receiver, who then must work on interpretations to reduce uncertainty.

When and How to Use Trade-offs

Trade-offs are when the aforementioned strategies are combined in various ways, balancing one kind of risk against another. I have already mentioned explicitation as an example of trade-offs, but there are several more general models of how this can work, depending on the positive or negative perspectives. A positive example would be the Chinese version of *Coca-Cola* as 可口可乐 which phonetically imitates the English ('kě kǒu kě lè') and uses characters that mean something like 'to permit the mouth to be able to rejoice' (Pym and Hu 2024). If the phonetics came closer to the English, the semantics would suffer; and if the semantics were made more appealing, the phonetics would suffer. A trade-off of this kind scores positively on two otherwise opposed value scales.

A classic negative model is the use of sprinkler systems for fire prevention in office blocks: fire and water both cause damage, but the damage from water is less, so we choose to take that risk. How can this be applied to translation? A simple example would be postediting a fairly good machine-translation output. If you keep going backward and forward between the start text and the translation, you miss the textual flow and coherence, but if you do not look at the start text at all, you miss mistakes. A pragmatic trade-off is usually to read the translation as a text and then go back to the original in cases of doubt. A trade-off with different values is to revise the translation comparatively all the way and then read the whole translation as a stand-alone text (thus completing a 'review,' according to some nomenclatures): you gain in error detection and textual quality, but you lose on the time taken.

Trade-offs can concern other aspects of the translation workflow. Imagine you are choosing someone to revise a translation that has been done from Japanese to English. If you select a reviser whose first language is Japanese, they might pick up all the nuances on the start side but miss some on the target side, and vice versa if the reviser's first language is English. Which choice will cause the less damage? It probably depends on the nature of the text, the purpose of the translation, where cooperation is sought, and how the particular translation culture has evolved.

There are also intriguing paradoxes in these trade-offs. Monacelli and Punzo (2001) note that in military interpreting, the hierarchy of linguistic authority is structured in such a way that the linguists who certify the equivalence of a rendition are those who sit behind desks. That means that the further one is from the battlefield, the more authoritative the translation, despite all the lessons from pragmatics about meaning depending on immediate situations. A similar instance of a trade-off between experience and control can be found, at least on paper, in the Tokyo War Crimes Trial, where disagreements over translations were resolved by a committee comprising an American military officer (representing the court), a Japanese American lawyer (representing the prosecution), and a Japanese journalist (representing the defense). The head language arbiter was nevertheless an American who was the least linguistically competent of all. Takeda (2010) did not detect any instances of biased decisions, but the need for control as well as competence is made clear enough in the institutional structure.

A strangely similar problem appeared with public arguments (especially from Deul 2021) that translators of Amanda Gorman's poem *The Hill We Climb* (2021) should be black artists who work with the spoken word. In this case, it seems racial identity could trump professional expertise, although it must still be possible to have something of both at the same time – as was unfortunately forgotten in much of the debate that followed.

Most situations involving time pressure also call for some kind of trade-off rather than simply taking risks. I mentioned the 'Too late to leave' message, where a bushfire is approaching and time is of the essence. If we use machine translation for the texts, we know there are likely to be problems in some languages with the second-person *you*, as in: "You are in danger and need to act immediately to survive" or "You should move indoors." As mentioned, this second person creates problems for machine translations into languages that make a distinction between the formal and the informal variants. To avoid the problem, we could prepare pre-edited templates in which the original English texts simply do not use the second person, as in: "Given the danger to life, action must be taken immediately" or "Everyone should move indoors."

On the other hand, I noted that the second person is generally recommended in this kind of message, at least in English, because it conveys the urgency of taking individual action. This means that if we adopt the above pre-editing, we avoid the hazard of inconsistent second persons, but we lose the presumed benefit of directly addressing the person who must take the action. This is like the choice between water damage and fire damage. Retaining the second person, at least for the most vital instructions, would be like accepting the consequences of installing water sprinklers. What you win on the swings is presumed to be less than what you lose on the roundabouts.

As it happens, our current technologies provide a solution to this problem: prepare the templates with the second person, run them through machine translation (hopefully with some overrides from translation memories and glossaries), and then control the second person by feeding the result through generative AI, specifying the reader in the prompt. When automated solutions are cheap (although there are environmental costs as well), there is no reason to stick with just one.

Something like this logic operates at a more banal level whenever two or more different solutions are given or compensatory elements are put in translators' notes, prefaces, or other secondary material. Some translation problems can only be solved by adding extensive information, but the added information comes at the cost of altering the form and register of the start text. In the case of literary translations, the latter values are sometimes considered paramount, so the added information is given elsewhere, in a footnote, endnote, glossary, preface, or critical article. The reader can find the information, the textual form is preserved, and the only downside is that the reader must work to find where the information has been put.

That said, the use of multiple solutions is not always straightforward. For instance, the original editions of Mark Twain's *Huckleberry Finn* contain what Americans cryptically call the 'n-word' when referring to African Americans. The word was in general usage at the time and had few of the extremely negative racialized values that it now carries in American English. So how should we translate Twain's English into contemporary languages, including contemporary English? If the edition is going to come anywhere near young readers, then none of the 'double presentation' solutions is going to work: I certainly do not remember seeing the word when I read *Huckleberry Finn* as a child. Omission is the order of the day, or a radical toning down. In a separate scholarly edition, we might nevertheless expect to see the word accompanied by appropriate notes. The beauty of electronic publishing is that separate editions are now relatively easy to produce; the risk is that they are all available to everyone.

Trade-offs can also be found in the reception of translations, whenever two or more opposed values are related in such a way that both can be achieved at the same time but to varying degrees. A case studied by Ke Hu (in Pym and Hu 2024) is the reception of name translations in the eighteenth-century Chinese family saga *Hong Lou Meng* (紅樓夢), translated as *Dream of the Red Chamber* and *The Story of the Stone*. The novel has more than 700 characters, some of whose names have semantic content that is important for the narrative. For example, a beautiful and clever woman is named 熙凤 (Hsi-feng), which literally means 'splendid phoenix.' But if you just call her *Phoenix* in the translation, you lose the Chinese quality, and if you call her *Hsi-feng*, you lose the semantic values. This is where translators seek all kinds of trade-offs, using different strategies for different names and deploying translator notes when necessary. Comments on Goodreads and Amazon indicate that readers appreciate a certain number of translated names for the main characters, which help them follow the story and indicate when the names have a functional meaning, but having too many translations and explanations simply adds to the confusion. If mixed translation strategies can address the basic criteria of narrative value and cultural location, at least to some extent, all goes reasonably well. But when the Oxford translator David Hawkes systematically uses *French* for the names of prostitutes or sing-song girls, and then *Latin* for the religious characters, many readers feel that the Chinese location has been interfered with – French and Latin had little place in eighteenth-century China, after all. The delicate balance of the trade-off is thus broken for those readers, exposing Hawkes' strategy as being particularly risk-taking. Although some readers go along with the game, many do not.

Something similar was found in Bei Hu's research on the ways Australians received English translations of Chinese foreign affairs discourse (Hu 2022). For most readers, positive values were associated both with understandability (often through adaptation) *and* with the Chinese location of the discourse (often through nonadaptation). Much as one might suppose that adaptation should lead to readers' appreciation and acceptance, Hu found that some readers reacted negatively to a translated discourse that did not sound like the foreignness they expected of China – the adaptations could go too far.

The logic of trade-offs is instructive in that it challenges many of the sweeping theories that propose just one kind of solution to each translation problem. Risk management rarely conforms to absolutist principles. Further, when trade-offs are attempted but do not work, what is potentially lost is a value of extreme importance in risk management: trust in the translator.

4 Trust as Risk Management

This section focuses on trust as the social glue that enables cooperation to extend over time. If mutual benefits are to be found, then each participant must predict and then trust that the others will respond within appropriate limits. Here I mainly consider the ways translators are trusted as individuals and sometimes as a profession.

The Kind of Trust That Is Pertinent to Translation

The word 'trust' covers numerous different meanings, only some of which are intimately related to risk. If I trust the sun will rise tomorrow, that expectation is based on accrued routine. It might be wrong, but there is not much I can do about it. There is no decision to take and therefore no risk of me or anyone else being wrong. Dead, probably, but not wrong. There is no risk management involved.

Other kinds of routine produce expectations where a decision can be taken. If I trust that the airplane I board will not crash, there is not a lot I can do about that either, but I *can* choose not to get on the plane. To that extent, the act of trusting concerns both routine and risk. I *choose* to trust that the airline, the pilot, and the weather reports are all reasonably reliable. I know there are risks, but I assume they are of less consequence than what I benefit from the flight. I might also choose to trust the science that calculates the carbon footprint of the flight, where I similarly estimate that the hazards are less than the benefits. Do I check the details of all those calculations? Not at all. I decide to trust them based on reasons that are far from calculated: others trust the flight too (if I were alone on the plane I would be worried); the pilots and crew wear special uniforms (the pseudo-military allure tells me that special skills have been tested somewhere); and I have boarded many flights without a crash (accrued routine still counts for something). Those factors do not remove the risk, but they enable me to manage it intuitively – in the weeks following a publicized plane crash, the risks are generally thought to be greater and there is less social trust, even though the statistical risk will be almost the same (Kahneman 2011). When I get on the plane, the kind of trust that I enact involves doing something based on calculations that I do not control. I therefore mentally bracket out all the aspects I cannot calculate, making trust a classical leap of faith (Möllering 2001) necessary for the psychological reduction of complexity (Luhmann 1968). This kind of trust thereby becomes "a solution for specific problems of risk" (Luhmann 1988: 95).

How does this relate to translation? Whenever the receiver of a translation does not know the foreign language, they are invited to trust the translator in much the same way as I trust the pilot of the plane I board. I say 'much the same' because translation involves the added risk of betrayal, of someone perhaps working for the other side. The common territory remains the way the act of trusting mentally brackets out the parts we cannot control, the skills of the trusted party are not reproduced by the trustor, and there is always the available decision to not get on board (or not receive the translation) and to choose another flight (go for a retranslation, if one is available).

I insist that this kind of trust involves routine and thus familiarity but is not reducible to numbers. Approaches to translation that involve frequency-based norms, corpus linguistics, big data, or some forms of complexity theory tend to overlook the psychology of risk and the special role of trust in managing risk. This kind of trust cannot be firmly grounded in reason, knowledge, or repetition-based trial and error.

Credibility Risk

To operate as guides to the foreign, translators need to be trusted by their clients and end users. Loss of this credibility is the prime risk they face. This can be seen in cases where intercultural communication fails.

In Judith Raigal's study of court cases in Barcelona, there comes a point where a judge starts to doubt the interpreter's command of English, since the judge assumes she herself knows legal English (this does not happen in cases where Romanian or Chinese is the foreign language). One of the instances concerns whether one *robs* or *steals* a mobile phone; another is whether the police can *detain* a suspect (the judge thinks the verb is wrong in English). In this series of trivial disagreements about the English language, which neither the judge nor the interpreter wholly commands, the tension escalates until the interpreter is dismissed from the court (Pym, Raigal-Aran, & Bestué Salinas 2023). Once the rot sets in, there is no stopping it.

How is it possible to trust a translator if you do not know the foreign language? On the evidence from the court, the act of trusting is actually made easier by the trustor's absence of alternatives, in this case, their lack of language skills. Recourse is usually made to all the signals of trustworthiness that *surround* the individual translator: their educational and professional qualifications, the agency or publisher they work for, the other people who trust them (perhaps a list of clients), the way they write or speak (European Commission interpreters used to have accents from Oxford or Cambridge), or the knowledge they display when speaking about translation (as in Kudos points on the translation job platform ProZ).

Such deceptively ephemeral signals are extremely important for the development of translation as a profession. In a situation where there are no such signals, the client does not know whom to trust. They are thereby condemned to select a translator at random, which incurs a higher probability of receiving a poor-quality translation. In accordance with the neoclassical economic theory of adverse selection (Akerlof's seminal 1970 paper concerns the market for second-hand cars, applied to translation in Chan 2008), a high probability of low quality will lead to lower rates of pay for translators; the lower pay then forces highly skilled translators out of the market; this further reduces the quality delivered by the remaining translators; and so on until rates of pay are so low that no one can make a living from translation and no client is going to trust a translation anyway. There are indications that something like this might have been happening in parts of the translation market in recent years. The solution, according to neoclassical economics, is to institutionalize signals of trustworthiness, in the same way that used-car dealers were obliged to provide visible information on the condition of each car. Once those signals enable some translators to be trusted more than others, it becomes possible to pay for their higher trustworthiness. The rates of pay and the likelihood of high quality then increase in those parts of the market, attracting talented translators, who not only stay in the market but might also prosper in niche sectors involving high-stakes cooperation.

I note in passing that trust in the translator is often confounded with relative trust in the various parties involved in the translation: the publisher, other clients, the institution giving the signal of quality, right through to what is probably the most powerful transfer of trust signaling: recommendation by word of mouth. There can also be a certain transfer of trustworthiness from the institutional status of the message itself. When we were working on vaccination messaging in Melbourne (Pym & Hu 2022), we found that some communities were predisposed to trust official information and therefore tended to trust government-employed translators, whereas other communities tended to distrust both, as a simple halo effect. The difference mapped roughly onto the degree with which public institutions were trusted in the countries of origin. Of course, this kind of halo effect can be challenged, as when a highly trusted medical doctor translates the information given by a weakly trusted government. We have also found cases where translators from communities with traditionally low trust in government did not believe the vaccination information that they themselves were translating (Macreadie et al. 2025).

Halo effects similarly influence the workings of distrust. Studies on detention centers for asylum seekers in Ljubljana (Pokorn & Čibej 2018) and Leipzig (Fiedler & Wohlfarth 2018) report that some asylum seekers from low-trust communities view host-government interpreters with suspicion, preferring to use online machine translation instead. Suspicions about the intentions of governments thus become distrust of the government's qualified interpreters, as a kind of professionalization in reverse. In some cases, the distrust could be well-founded: Allaby (2018) reports cases where some interpreters may indeed have been spies working for the asylum-seekers' home governments.

Text Quality and the Ruse of Trust

The potential loss of credibility can have significant effects on risk-management strategies. It can affect, for example, the default supposition that an error in a low-stakes part of a text is of little consequence. An example would be the mixing of the formal and informal second persons, mentioned earlier, which is of no practical consequence for actionability but will nevertheless alert the receiver to the possibility that the translation has been done by an unskilled translator, or by several different translators, or by automated translation. That suspicion can lead to a low level of trust and in some cases to outright distrust. In that kind of situation, *any* error in *any* part of a text can be used to undermine the translator's credibility. And if loss of credibility is the translator's prime risk, if it is the worst thing that can happen, suspicions about trustworthiness can make all parts of the text high-stakes. In that kind of situation, translators are probably quite justified in distributing their efforts in a more even way, taking care to avoid errors at all levels. They turn to literalism and the strategies of risk aversion, or they run the text through several automatic quality assessments.

Does that mean that the theory of unequal effort distribution is wrong? It can certainly not presume universal applicability. There are, however, situations in which mediators build up high degrees of personal credibility, earning trust on multiple levels and between several communication partners. An example might be Pavel Palazhchenko, the Russian interpreter who reportedly knew more about nuclear nonproliferation than the series of Soviet presidents he worked for, or perhaps Zhang Lu, the star Chinese conference interpreter whose diplomatic skills at idiom-matching are apparently unquestioned. In those situations of high trust, translators have the relative freedom to distribute their efforts as they see fit, editing out or toning down the inconsequential parts of texts, and investing effort in the main points to be understood (Pym 2022). A level of credibility is required for those risk-taking strategies to be deployed.

Preferences for Thick or Thin Trust

A useful distinction can be made between thick trust, in which a person is trusted on several social levels or in several overlapping networks, and thin trust, where the person is only known and trusted on just one level, usually on the basis of professional qualifications (Putnam 2000; Hosking 2014, 46–49; applied to translation history in Rizzi, Lang, & Pym 2019). When a mafia boss trusts family, the trust is very thick, to the extent that any betrayal can be punished in very personal terms. But when a client or a receiver trusts a qualified translator, the trust can be so thin that any personal details of the translator are considered irrelevant. The ideal of professionalization assumes that thin trust is enough: all qualified translators are ideally assumed to work the same way, such that you take your text to *the* translator, just as you might take your health problems to *the* doctor. The development of that kind of thin trust has been a feature of most translation markets in industrial and postindustrial societies over the past fifty years or so, in parallel with the development of the language industry in some parts of the world. Both historical tendencies are often seen in positive terms.

Although these two kinds of trust are polarities on a continuum, their abstract differences enable us to consider the ways they interact with risk management.

In thin trust, credibility is effectively transferred to the *institution* that issues the professional qualification. If you trust that institution, you trust all translators that have its accreditation. In thick trust, on the other hand, routine, familiarity, and visibility play much larger roles, allowing for a more robust kind of relationship. Thin trust might be upset by the inherent variability of translation – a naïve receiver will ask why qualified translators do not all produce the same translation. Thick trust has an answer prepared: translators are different people, so they translate differently.

Calls for the complete professionalization of translation tend to focus on thin trust alone. They seek professional accreditation, a uniform code of ethics, and specialized academic qualifications. All those thin signals can theoretically lead from market disorder to the ideals of 'protection and licensure' (Ju 2009: 120; Pym et al. 2013: 76). At the same time, those moves are strategically outflanked by the series of industrial standards, especially following ISO 17100:2015, that shift the focus of trust from the product to the workflow that leads to the product, thereby inviting trust in the company that subscribes to the standard and, beyond that, in the institutional system of industrial standards. Thin trust need no longer be in the human translator, or at least, not in any illusion that the translator is working without automation.

At the same time, a certain critique of alienation can lament both professionalization and industrial standards as the loss of thick trust, particularly in workflows where translators work for agencies, never see the paying client, and thereby typically have little information on the end user of the text. Abdallah and Koskinen (2007) see this as eroding the trust relationship, which they claim can only properly operate when "the perspectives and interests of each stakeholder are addressed, knowledge is shared, and information is clear" (2007: 140). The problem with this view, at least from the perspective of an epistemology based on uncertainty, is that absolute clarity is not only impossible but would also remove the need for any kind of strong trust or indeed risk management – the relationship would merely involve routine and familiarity.

A counterargument can be based on Granovetter (1973), who proposed that what he termed 'weak ties' where people are related only by professionalism are very necessary in order for fragmented social groups to share information and seek a common purpose. In our social-media echo chambers where we only ever encounter people who think like us, we build up ever thicker trust relationships within the group, or indeed within our language. Thin trust in professionals can at least ensure that information can flow from group to group, language to language, and be accorded credibility.

Both thick and thin trust can be useful in the search for cooperation, each in a different way.

Thin Trust and the Invisibility of the Receiver

There is a strong view among translation scholars, particularly in the wake of German-language *Skopos* theory of the 1980s, that translators should adapt their texts to specific purposes and specific readerships. That view is becoming stronger with the advent of generative AI, which seems to be reasonably good at straight translation tasks, usefully suggestive for the more adaptive tasks, and makes mistakes that are notoriously hard to spot. Where will translators find employment in this scenario? One answer is that we can turn to rewriting, adaptation, transcreation, and content development – any number of terms to show that translators can do more than translate ... and should be well paid for it.

If that vision is to work, at least three things seem to be required. First, the translator's activity should ideally involve high-stakes texts in high-stakes situations. If not, it will be much cheaper for a client to trust that automation will provide something good enough – as many people are doing these days for everyday translations. Second, the kind of trust needed for the more adaptive and creative tasks would seem to be of an especially thick kind, where a lot is known about the translator, who becomes an individual paid to work with a certain individuality. And third, the translator must receive information on the end-user of the translation and the effects that the text is supposed to have. Without those three elements in place, the image of the highly paid creative adapter of texts may well be little better than a pipe dream.

There is no easy revolution here. When Suojanen et al. (2015) argue the case for 'user-centered translation' that involves adaptation of this kind, they implicitly assume that those three elements are in place, even though at some points they admit that lack of information can make the translator's audience more like an anonymous hypothesis (Suojanen et al. 2015: 26, 136–137). When the purpose and the readership are in doubt, when there are no rewards for taking risks, and when the translator is not trusted to take risks anyway, one should not be surprised to find translators defaulting to a risk-averse approach.

This is not to suggest there is no social space for highly adaptive and creative translators, which have always had their niche markets. I merely point out the historical forces that work against it. The process of professionalization that has been going on for fifty years or more, depending on the society, focuses on thin trust only and goes hand in hand with restrictive codes of ethics based on accuracy to the text, in many cases as an unreasonable generalization of what is required in the legal domain. The more you have models of professionalization based on thin trust, the harder it will be to gain the thick trust necessary for adaptive translation.

The Special Role of Distrust

When you set out to study trust relationships, the main methodological problem is that trust itself is mostly invisible. If there is a strong trust relationship between a translator and a client, then they have no reason to verbalize the fact.

The different kinds of trust can nevertheless be identified empirically by considering instances where trust fails or is questioned – situations in which otherwise invisible trust relationships break down.

This brings up the nature of distrust, which in the domain of translation I think should be regarded as something more than the absence or failure of trust. In interactions that concern a language and a culture that a client or end-user does not know, the most extreme risk is that the mediator could be working for the other side, whose language and culture they partly share by definition. Distrust in this situation would be "an actor's assured expectation of *intended harm* from the other" (Lewicki, McAllister, & Bies 1998: 446). That is, it involves a perceived risk of betrayal.

That does not mean that there need be actual betrayal. In many cases where trust is reduced, the low level of trust can be attributed to suspected incompetence. This is what we found in the Barcelona courts where two interpreters were removed from their functions: they were suspected of making too many language mistakes, not of actually working for the defendants. Distrust of the stronger kind nevertheless surfaced when we studied COVID translations in Australia, especially in communities that did not trust the government, did not trust the government's information, and therefore did not trust the translators who relayed that information. As mentioned, we also found cases of translators themselves not trusting the texts they were translating (Macreadie et al. 2025). Once distrust starts in a system, it can spread quickly: "through a sort of halo-effect the diffuse culture of distrust is apt to expand toward interpersonal dealings as well as relations with outsiders" (Sztompka 1997: 11). This means that distrust of the translator may in many cases be riding on deeper distrust of the institutions with which the translator is associated. Either way, once the translator reaches the territory of negative credibility, of distrust in the sense of suspected treason, there is not much risk management can do.

5 Risks in Automated Translation

Not so many years ago, anyone giving a public talk on translation could get a few cheap laughs by citing errors from machine translation: 'Please leave your values at the front desk' (reportedly in a Paris hotel), 'Drop your trousers here' (at a Bangkok dry cleaner's), and so on. As the laughs subsided, the expert would assure us that machines would never be able to translate – translation was a complex task that would always require a human professional.

Those mistakes are now quite rare; the guffaws are now more like nervous twitters. When professionals are rendering much less than one percent of the words translated in the world (Pym & Torres-Simón 2021), the people who were once laughing are now likely to be using translation technologies themselves to communicate with that hotel in Paris or the dry cleaner's in Bangkok, or they are turning to machine translation on a daily basis as a quick bilingual dictionary. Language automation was once so error-prone as to involve serious risk-taking (the Austin Powers meme was 'I see you're using Google Translate ... I live danger also like'); it is now being trusted to some degree by millions for routine everyday communication. What has happened to our risk management?

This section considers the communication risks presented by a set of technologies that can be grouped together as 'automation': translation memory suites, neural machine translation, and generative artificial intelligence (large language models). It argues that the traditional prejudices against automation need to be overcome and that certain modes of automation are entering into a new kind of trust relationship.

Different Technologies, Different Kinds of Risk

The *auto* part of 'automation' means that something happens by itself, without human intervention. That can bring greater reliability (machines do what you tell them to do) but also a certain lack of control (machines are restricted by limited data, unclear instructions, and the nature of language as a set of imperfect clues). Mistakes happen, but they do not happen in the same way in all technologies.

Translation memory suites, for instance, record previous translations of a sentence, so that if the same or a similar sentence is to be translated again, we can see what was done in the past and then choose to repeat or modify the previous rendition. When the technology is used to provide translation proposals by drawing from its database, there are no special risks involved, at least when the context is similar. When, however, clients or project managers use translation memories to oblige the translator to accept fixed translations and terminology, the risk is that sentences are translated as if any new context were always exactly the same as the previous context. In technical texts with highly predictable contexts, that may be of marginal concern. In many other situations, however, the technology contradicts the basic message of pragmatics: meaning depends on the relation between utterance and context.

Machine translation has been a far more adventurous affair, at least prior to the neural models introduced around 2016. Imperfect algorithms worked on limited training data, giving results that very much depended on how regulated the texts and contexts were. As with translation memory systems, the technology could be quite reliable when in a constrained domain: rule-based machine translation was used for French-English weather reports in Canada from 1977. However, when that Canadian system was extended to the translation of maintenance manuals for aircraft, it was instructed to *omit* any sentence for which complete information was not available in the grammars and dictionaries (Macklovitch 1984). If you are working on aircraft, omission is better than a guess. As it happened, there were so many omissions and the costs were so high that the aircraft project was abandoned.

When translation memory systems began to incorporate machine-translation feeds, the translator had a choice: to work from the stored previous translations or to accept or modify the machine translations. The translation memories were home-produced and thus generally safer, so the translator would only turn to the machine translation in cases of doubt or when in need of inspiration. Interestingly, one of the relative advantages of machine translation was that when it was wrong, it was often *wildly* wrong ('hallucinations' were proposals unrelated to the context), whereas the translation-memory proposals would always be similar, requiring that effort be invested in repairing fuzzy matches. Machine translations could be so wrong that the translator could save time and avoid risks by wiping them away and translating from scratch.

The use of deep learning in neural machine translation from around 2016 means that there are now far fewer hallucinations in that strong sense, at least for languages with large electronic resources. The comparison these days tends to be with generative artificial intelligence, where translations are like those of machine translation but are often more fluent and coherent, making the detection of errors an even more effortful process. The nature of hallucinations has also shifted: now the term tends to refer to the presentation of plausible but erroneous references, invented examples, and spurious precedents. A lawyer who relied on ChatGPT to argue in court reportedly presented a list of prior legal cases of which none could actually be found (Weiser 2023). The stakes were high and the outcome was duly cringe-worthy for the lawyer, but the problem concerned more than translation.

Consumer Protection

Given the persistence of hallucinations – now in the form of difficult-to-detect lies rather than off-the-charts stabs-in-the-dark – most generative AI services add warnings whenever a response concerns a legal, financial, or medical matter. You are advised to consult a paid lawyer, financial advisor, or medical professional. I have asked OpenAI and Google to provide the same advice in the case of translations, which can concern similar risks. I am still waiting for a reply.

A more general kind of consumer protection concerns the idea of labeling translations to indicate their provenance, in the same way as food products are labeled. A simple proposal, currently championed by Alan Melby (see the website tranquality.info) is to distinguish between UMT (Unedited Machine Translation) and BRT (Bilingually Reviewed Translation). The difference between the two is the intervention of a reviser who knows the two languages. The hope is presumably that mention of a human-in-the-loop will inspire greater trust than is likely to be accorded to the raw output of a machine, which is assumed to involve high risks.

This proposal is appealing because it offers just two terms, which stand a chance of being recognized and remembered. There are numerous further distinctions that could be added, especially the various degrees of human intervention (fully human, single revision, revision and review, etc.) and the variable criteria for who is qualified to do the revising (academic studies, professional exams, years of experience, etc.). And then there are algorithms that can do a bilingual revision without the intervention of a human. The labels could become as complicated as you like. It is good to stay with just two.

Personally, I nevertheless find the proposed labels opaque and conceptually problematic. Nowadays we need some reference to AI, not just machine translation, so I would propose a simple 'AI' label, insisting that machine translation is and has always been an instance of artificial intelligence. On the other side of the equation, if the important factor is *trust* in the human, I would focus more squarely on that trust function: 'certified translation' might do the trick, perhaps even using real words instead of an acronym. It does not necessarily matter what the human translator has actually done. What counts is the fact that a trustworthy person has signed off on the result.

Risks of Data Breaches

Another kind of risk is more technical. Ever since the use of online translation-memory systems in the 1990s, I have been telling my students *never* to upload their clients' confidential documents to any third-party site, which would include any of the online automation services. The risk of data leakage is assumed to be of greater consequence than any of the advantages gained.

Now, after some thirty years of giving that warning, I am starting to wonder why I can find no court cases where someone is sued for plagiarism or intellectual property infringement because of online automatic translation. Have I been propagating an urban legend? Am I being as overly cautious as the film companies that force their subtitlers to work without seeing the film?

Most of the online translation services operate with fine print that says the company will use your data to improve their systems – no 'free' online service is ever entirely free – but they usually promise the data will not be given to anyone else. And then there is sometimes further fine print that absolves the company from responsibility if the data are disclosed. There is a report of the company translate.com making customers' sensitive documents available online (Tomter, Zondag, & Skiller 2017, with thanks to Sara Horcas for the reference). That problem, though, was due to incompetent data management, not to anything specific to translation as such.

The lesson is nevertheless clear and commonsensical: do not give sensitive data to anyone you do not trust entirely. Of course, the more you pay for the service, the more you might have grounds to trust it (Canfora & Ottmann 2020). The lasting solution is to develop in-house systems for translation automation, which means that you trust yourself.

Does that imply that no online translation system should ever be used? Not necessarily. Lyu et al. (2023) suggest the risks can be mitigated by anonymizing any text that is uploaded anywhere. That sounds like tedious work in exchange for fairly superficial protection. A smarter solution would seem to be to use online translation systems only to solve juicy problems, uploading no more than a paragraph or so at a time. I regularly do this on DeepL, where the drop-down menus provide a wonderful sandpit for working on the most complicated issues.

The Special Risks of Language Automation

Given that the aforementioned risks make their way into public discourse and are habitually magnified without any empirical testing, neural machine translation and generative artificial intelligence are often thought to be highly prone to error and therefore untrustworthy. And yet free online automated translation accounts for more than 99 percent of the world's translated words (not necessarily *read* words!) (Pym and Torres-Simón 2021), so they are presumably being trusted in many situations. Their special risks would correspond to some kind of 'good-enough' usage, usually of the 'better than nothing' kind. The situations where the free services are used commonly involve such low stakes that a human translator would not have been employed in the past, so it cannot be assumed that automation is now taking work away from humans. The choice is mostly between the machine and nothing, not between the machine and a human.

Andrew Chesterman has claimed that "[t]ranslators, in order to survive as translators, must be trusted by all parties involved, both as a profession and individually. [...] Without this trust, the profession would collapse, and so would its practice" (1997: 181, 182). But what happens to trust when the text comes to the receiver with the backing of *no* profession and *no* individual translator? There would appear to be a kind of risk-taking here that can operate in the absence of a trustworthy person or identifiable profession.

As mentioned, I have been part of a team investigating the use of automation for emergency messages: warnings about bushfires, sharks, and the like (reported in Hajek et al. 2024). We found that machine translation and generative AI make mistakes, sometimes very high-stakes mistakes. One particular problem was the clause *If you are caught in fire in your car*, which was followed by specific instructions including *position the car facing the fire*. With those instructions, the reader of the English text can parse the clause as 'If you are caught in fire [in your car]' – you are in your car, the fire is around the car, and you cannot drive away safely. Automated translation, though, does not have enough information to make those connections. The clause was translated into Spanish, Chinese, Italian, and other languages as *If your car is on fire*: 'Si se incendia su automóvil,' '如果您的车着' (my thanks to Hao Yu). It was parsed as 'If you are caught in [fire in your car],' which presumably was the most statistically probable interpretation of that isolated clause. Those automated translations rendered the subsequent instructions nonsensical – it is hard to park a car if it is on fire. In December 2023, this erroneous translation was given by Google Translate, DeepL, GPT3.5, Google Gemini, and Microsoft Copilot. A few months later, in May 2024, some of those systems still made the mistake, but others had changed to a word-for-word rendition of the English, particularly when the subsequent instructions were present. In Spanish, this gave *Si se encuentra atrapado en su automóvil en fuego*, which back-translates as 'If you are caught in your car in fire.' The meaning is not immediately obvious, but at least the sentence can be parsed in both ways. Part of the risk is thereby transferred to the reader, who is called upon to interpret the sentence, probably in quite a hurry.

I tested this machine translation on twenty-nine speakers of Spanish, giving them a choice of four actions to take. In the case of the first translation ('if your car is on fire'), only twelve of them gave the right answer – quite a few lives could have been lost. With the literal version, however, almost all of them interpreted it correctly, relying on common sense rather than what the text said. True, the answers took a long time to come (we did this as an online questionnaire), which could similarly be fatal when a bushfire is approaching. More interestingly, when I asked readers how they were able to make sense of this and similar infelicities in the machine translation, one answered: "It's obviously a machine translation, so I trust what the author is saying but not what the translation says." And when I asked if this was normal: "We get this kind of thing all the time."

This reaction suggests a very particular kind of risk management when the receiver is aware they are interpreting an automated translation. Precisely because they have a *low* level of trust in the translation (although not distrust, since machines do not usually betray), they interpret the text on the basis of situational expectations – what would sound right in the situation, not what the text actually says. We have found that some receivers of translations, particularly younger users, have a highly developed capacity to overlook the surface level of the text, to bracket out items that seem not to fit in, and generally to process defective machine translations with reasonable efficiency. We find this not only in emergency messaging, where a wrong interpretation could have fatal consequences, but also in machine-translated subtitles of online drama, where there are often online discussions of translation problems for those who are interested (Qiu & Pym 2024). This kind of low-trust reception might be reasonably new in some of its technological dimensions, especially the online comments and discussions, but is by no means a novel interpretative skill. We use it all the time, for example, when conversing with four-year-olds or perhaps with foreign speakers who have intelligent things to say but do not always find the right words with which to say them. We trust the intentions, as far as they can be construed, not what is said.

When generative artificial intelligence translates, it generally performs as well or better than neural machine translation for high-resource languages, but with a degree of textual fluency that is more inviting to text-based trust. With machine translation, the receiver can activate a regime of low-trust reception. With generative AI, that seems harder to do. Even when a reader suspects the translation is unreliable in parts, it is more difficult to identify those parts. To return to the problem of the second person in emergency messaging, the machine translations jump between the formal and the informal, alerting the reader that they should interpret with care. The generative AI translations, on the other hand, are wholly formal or wholly informal, depending on the prompts, leaving the receiver with fewer clues as to the trustworthiness of the translation.

There is much to be discovered about the effects of generative AI. On the one hand, as mentioned, the greater fluency can encourage unwarranted trust. On the other, generative AI systems can offer multiple different translations when asked to do so. Sometimes the prompt has to insist that the second translation must be different, but Google Gemini, for example, seems to assume you were not happy with the first translation and so it offers something less literal. And if you ask it to translate many times, the translations move further and further away from the original text. It is then up to the receiver to determine the translation most suitable for their situation. It may seem that the system is taking increasing risks, but since the user then has to decide, risk has effectively been moved downstream.

This is of interest because, if and when the receiver is thereby made aware of the inherent variability of translation, that awareness should run counter to the trustworthiness encouraged by the fluency of the text. The high-trust reception regime activated by the one-off translation could be compensated for by the reduced forms of trust that ensue from seeing several different translations. Much will depend on how people are trained to use these technologies. If, as I hope, generative AI responses are approached as sources of suggestions rather than as authorities, as a way to augment rather than replace language skills, they could invite the low-trust reception regime that we have found in the use of machine translations.

How to Work with Language Automation

In our report on machine translation for emergency messaging (Hajek et al. 2024), we did *not* recommend the use of raw machine translation. The time savings offered by automation in emergency situations were obviously considerable, but so were some of the risks. Questionnaires and focus-group discussions showed that mixes of the formal and informal second person detracted from the perceived trustworthiness of the text, while the 'car on fire' translation blocked sense-making for a small set of instructions. In the same document on bushfires, the English instruction 'Try to position your car towards the approaching fire' came out as '尝试将汽车停在靠近火场的位置,' which back-translates as 'Try to park your car close to a fire.' Not great advice! Just a couple of cases like that should indicate that, in high-stakes messaging, the risks of raw machine translation can outweigh the advantages. As researchers, we did not want to recommend a measure that could have fatal consequences.

At the same time, one should not leave whole communities without any chance of timely translations in an emergency. In the spirit of trade-offs, we therefore outlined several measures that can be taken to mitigate the risks of machine translation:

> *Pre-editing*: If the start text is rewritten in a very explicit way, many of the errors are effectively eliminated before they occur. In the case of the 'car on fire' text, it was enough to rewrite the English as *If you are in your car and you cannot escape the fire*. And the 'position your car' problem was solved by rewriting the start text as *Park the car with the front towards the fire that is coming towards you*. Yu Hao and I did this together, pre-editing the English for translations into Spanish and Chinese, producing English texts that were

machine-translation-friendly. The resulting texts also turned out to fare better in the machine translations into Greek and Dari. This means that, even when pre-editing is not possible for a specific language pair, similar effects can be obtained by making the start texts as explicit as possible, avoiding local expressions, writing short sentences, avoiding syntactic inversions, and so on. Application of these measures becomes part of controlled authoring. The texts may not read very naturally, but they produce very few errors in the passage through machine translation.

Translated templates: About halfway through our research, we discovered our clients had templates for all the emergency messages, given that emergencies are rare but recurrent. Each new message was made by selecting the appropriate text chunks, filling in the blank spaces, and adding information when necessary. Since those templates exist independently of any time constraint, they should be translated by qualified professionals into the main languages at risk (applying some of the principles of medical triage, see Pym 2023b). Those translations should then be used to generate translation memories and glossaries, which can then be fed into translation-memory suites where they can override a machine-translation feed. Not many problems should remain.

Postediting: When raw machine translations are corrected, the process is called 'postediting,' as opposed to the 'pre-editing' that happens prior to the passage through machine translation. When there is time, all raw machine translations should be checked and corrected by a qualified professional. And if there is *not* much time, then the postediting should focus on issues of actionability, ensuring that the right actions will be taken. When this process is combined with pre-editing, the risks of error are reduced very considerably.

Revision in generative AI systems: Machine-translation systems basically work from databases of what translators have done in the past; generative AI systems pay attention to what target-language speakers will most probably say in the specified context. This means that the resulting translations can be quite different, although the judgments of quality are currently inconclusive: machine translation seems to perform better for low-resource languages, whereas generative AI systems are more fluent for high-resource languages. The real benefits of AI systems such as ChatGPT or Gemini (there are many more, with many names that will keep evolving) come when a particular purpose or receiver has to be specified and some adaptation or reworking is necessary. As mentioned, in our work on emergency messaging, the machine translations into Spanish, Greek, and Chinese all had trouble with the second person ('you'), which has formal and informal forms in all those languages but not in English. This meant that the raw machine translation outputs were all over the place, wandering between the formal and informal registers for no apparent reason. A quick solution was to have the translations corrected by a generative AI system, where it is easy to specify a formal or informal readership.

Contact persons: As we worked on the emergency messaging, we became aware that the various branches of Australia's Country Fire Authority not only put out messages but also have lists of people, with telephone numbers, who can receive the message and pass it on to others – like social media but without the technology. Those networks are in place already, although the people are not selected on the basis of language skills. To ensure that a machine translation is understood, a logical preparation would therefore be to identify and contact suitable bilinguals in each community at risk. Those people can then use their skills to provide support and clear up misunderstandings – without anyone assuming that they are unpaid and unqualified translators. Such people are ideally closer to the end users and thus more likely to be trusted (Cadwell 2019), which in turn means that the message is more likely to be trusted.

Can raw machine translation be used for high-stakes communication? It is certainly not advisable unless some or all of these above measures are taken. Then again, most of those measures can be taken well prior to any actual emergency. Further, many of them can be combined. If we suppose that urgency is a prime criterion in this translation workflow, then that value can be positioned with respect to the relative risks of a wrong action being taken ('actionability'). Figure 1 is a very rough attempt to map out the various options we have been looking at for those two variables. It suggests that the use of a human translator (an 'unaided professional') will give high actionability but will take a long time. At the other end, raw machine translation will give high speed but low (perhaps fatally low) actionability. The important point is that, in between those two extremes, there are many trade-off options, most of which can be combined with each other. Once you are aware of those additional measures, there is no reason to exile automation from the field of high-stakes communication.

One hastens to add that many other values can enter into the trade-offs here. The actual calculations might include factors such as social and economic costs, stylistic quality, and available electronic resources for the languages concerned. Even so, the automation of translation should be part of whatever trade-offs are sought.

Risk Assessment and Playing the Long Game

Kahneman's prospect theory (2011) is full of questions like the following: Would you rather have a 90 percent chance of winning $100 or a 10 percent chance of winning $10,000? Most people go for the first option, and so might most translators, if indeed they tend to be risk averse. Play it safe and cherish your winnings! But a professional gambler would logically go for the second option, which should bring far higher rewards in the long run – that is, if and

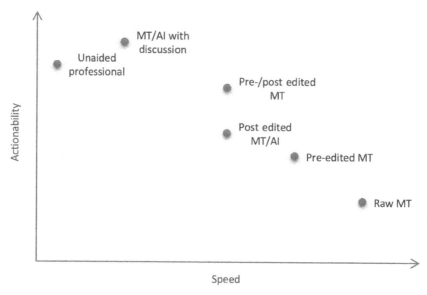

Figure 1 Trade-off positions with different workflows for emergency messaging.

when the bet can be placed a fair number of times. The risk-averse player only mentally sees the consequences of one bet; a gambler sees the longer view. But does that mean that the professional gambler is therefore taking higher risks? Yes and no. The example involves the same sense of risk but in different mental frames.

When translators look at the outputs of automated translation (be it machine translation or generative AI), they are remarkably skilled at zooming in on the mistakes and lamenting that risks have been taken. This is precisely what I have done with the bushfire text here, picking out and analyzing the main problematic sentences. To avoid those isolated errors, at least on a very local view, it is far better to take the safer bet and go with a fully human translation.

The industrial evaluation of automated translations does not operate at all like that. The evaluation metrics take habitually huge quantities of text and measure various kinds of edit distances (the simplest being the edits required to turn a machine translation into a human-produced reference translation), giving a score for the text taken as a whole. Quality becomes a question of statistics, the result of placing bets for large numbers of sentences, as a professional gambler would do – one isolated error is of little statistical consequence if most of the other sentences are entirely correct, since what counts in terms of profits is the quantity of text, deadlines, and thus the results of multiple plays. This should explain why large translation companies invest far more in automation, evaluation, and postediting than individual translators tend to, and why they reap greater profits (ELIS Research 2024: 38–39). They place their major bets more like professional gamblers – although I admit that the analogy is flawed because there is no one instance when they win big-time, and they can and should also take out insurance for the few high-stakes errors that slip through.

There is a more fundamental mistake in the gambling analogy. The automated metrics and large-scale evaluations based on edit distances tend to assume that all pieces of language have basically the same value, so they can be added up like numbers – mathematical corpus linguistics tends to succumb to the same fallacy. As the bushfire example illustrates, different errors involve very different stakes, sometimes life-threatening, depending on the local contexts in which they occur. Words are not numbers, and the benefits of communication are not always numbers of dollars. Sometimes the local view and the corresponding risk aversion are what is required.

Generative AI and the Future Work of Translators

The virtual stagnation of global capitalism since 2008 has created a deep-seated need for a technological breakthrough, for something – anything! – that can start the wheels of international commerce turning again. That need is one way to understand the hype that has surrounded generative AI since 2022, with public discourse both praising and lamenting its superhuman capacities, including the capacity to translate, while very rarely pausing to collect any systematic evidence. In the face of that public discourse, the only sane attitude is to engage with the technologies, assess their virtues and vices empirically, and adjust as necessary. Many of the predicted risks turn out to be wildly overblown.

In terms of a narrow accuracy-based concept of translation, I have noted that generative AI is not a huge qualitative advance on neural machine translation, and it tends to perform considerably worse in languages with limited electronic resources. It can nevertheless help translators with a long list of additional language tasks (Pym & Hao 2024: 62–63) and to that extent should be viewed very positively. In terms of employment prospects for translators, the pertinent calculation should not concern comparing one technology against another. It has far more to do with the democratization of a profession's basic skills: compare what a non-translator can do with generative AI to what a professional translator can do with (or without) generative AI. The progress of translation automation means that, by 2030 or thereabouts, we will have no great need to train large numbers of translators in the skills of sentence-to-sentence equivalence production, at least not in societies and generations with widespread computer literacy and languages with large electronic assets. Nonprofessionals can do that part pretty well (just as everyone can sing, more or less); professionals can do it very well, and much more, in high-stakes situations (people still pay to hear others sing, and opera singers can be very well paid).

This means that professional translators will have to focus on the high-level skills that are difficult to democratize, in addition to correcting the mistakes of automation. They can become experts in the engineering of sensitive prompts, to be sure, and they can take over some of the more creative and spoken tasks that the technology is not yet good at. But more importantly, and more in the long term, those who are now translators can and should gain expertise in managing the new sets of risks and fears that ensue from the technology. Part of that goes beyond the field of narrow translation, branching into the domains of transcreation and content creation. But another part will stay close to the technology. When a client is aware of the probability of error but the output is so fluent that mistakes are hard to detect, then a translator can come in not just to make the necessary adjustments, but more functionally to certify that the translation is valid, in the same way as a notary does for legal documents. In this, the translator's stock in trade becomes not just high-level linguistic and communication skills, but now, crucially, the ability to gain and maintain trust.

That means we should be training experts who can manage the risks of automated translation in various ways: assuming some risks by authorizing translations, transferring other risks to the moment of reception when appropriate, and generating new, risk-taking content when properly paid to do so.

6 A Case for More Risk-Taking

My arguments about risk management have been predicated on the assumption that cooperation is the general goal of cross-cultural communication. Some may find it hard to understand how that possibly anodyne starting position can lead to a conclusion where translators are called upon to take *more risks*, but that is indeed my purpose here. Much depends, of course, on how well one understands cooperation.

Let me return to Venuti, particularly to the way he expounds the noble aims of his translation strategies:

> To redress the global hegemony of English, to interrogate American cultural and political values, to evoke the foreignness of the foreign text, an American literary translator must not be cooperative, but challenging, not simply communicative, but provocative as well. (Venuti 1998: 21)

I have much sympathy for that kind of save-the-world aim, which clearly involves taking risks. The formulation, however, leaves me perplexed. Why should 'cooperative' be the opposite of 'challenging'? Surely one can willingly engage in communication in order to be challenged, since the result of a good challenge is likely to be a gain on your starting position – and a lot of good humor can come from challenges along the way. And why should 'communication' axiomatically exclude 'provocation'? These are quite strange ways to use our most basic terms.

In this case, Venuti's attempted critique of cooperation stems from a more profound misunderstanding. Grice's 'cooperative principle' posits that the participants in a conversation orient their contributions in terms of what they think is "a common purpose or set of purposes, or at least a mutually accepted direction" (Grice 1975: 45). If that does not happen, there is quite simply no conversation. Grice does not talk about mutual benefits, but he does assume that the hope of some degree of shared purpose keeps the interaction going. Venuti, however, seems to think Grice requires "an ideal speech situation in which the interlocutors are on an equal footing" (1998: 22). Not so, at least on my reading of Grice – the ideal homogeneity is assumed in Saussure and Chomsky, but not in Grice. More worryingly, Venuti seems blissfully unaware of the way Grice's theory of conversational implicatures accounts for the ways speakers *flout* maxims and can thereby *challenge* each other at almost every turn. A metaphor ('You are the cream in my coffee') is an expression that *breaks* the maxim of truth; irony ('She is a fine friend') *flouts* the maxim of relevance (assuming there are reasons to believe she is not a friend), and so on. The mental acrobatics required to interpret such moves – at least when analyzed in logical terms – are much more exciting and engaging than Venuti's translated nineteenth-century Italian who falls into 'a funk.' True, Venuti's translation here flouts a maxim of historical verisimilitude and is thereby challenging, but it does so without enabling any coherent secondary meaning to be construed – perhaps other than an egoistic translator implying, 'Look at me!' Venuti's reviewer did not try to construe the implicature because there was no apparent gain to be sought. That is, the risk-taking did not correspond to identifiable rewards, only incredulity: "Is this guy for real?" True, also, the implicature might have worked for other readers, since there are many kinds of people out there. But when a high-risk translation strategy fails, you cannot simply blame your reviewer for not following your instructions. You must pay much closer attention to how cooperation works. Indeed, the strategies for a type of communication that is fruitfully challenging and provocative, which is what Venuti obviously wants, could be found in the intelligent and playful use of everyday implicatures. Many of the risk-taking strategies we need can be located in common conversation, if you know where to look. Cooperation is not fanciful, and linguistics is worth understanding.

In much the same way as Venuti wants to use translation to "redress the global hegemony of English" (a lot of work for a bit of archaic funk!), PEN America (2023) sees American translators as being "positioned to resist or to perpetuate neoliberal globalization and its attendant forms of cultural imperialism," just when the world's major economies have abandoned neoliberalism. That kind of aim is as noble as Venuti's and is similarly nebulous: it is hard to see how success or failure could be judged. Again, I have sympathy for the ambition, but the formulation is embarrassing. Does continued cultural imperialism mean American translators have failed? Is there any particular reversal of hegemony that translators might claim responsibility for? How could one calculate the risks of communicative failure? And why the binary 'for or against'? Are translators not allowed to envisage any other kinds of aims?

What is happening here is that theorists are signing up to general causes into which their efforts can disappear without any risk of critical assessment. As long as we support the right team, we cannot be judged to fail. In its finer moments, this approach subscribes to what is traditionally called a 'realist' view, where everyone is opposed to everyone else and the goal of each participant is to maximize their own power or wealth: you win or lose on the global battleground, and there is nothing in between. That seems to underlie the purposes expressed by these American translators, and it is probably the dominant or even hegemonic view in the more activist parts of translation studies these days. Sapiro (2014, 2019) correspondingly sees translations as soft-power weapons that dominant cultures use to extend their hegemony, such that resistance can only come from increased translations from subaltern languages or countries. Seen from that perspective, any talk of cooperation must be no more than a naïve masking of what is happening in the world. On the realist view, for those who *really* know, the only risk to be calculated is the probability that the good side loses power, wealth, or moral influence.

There is no easy way to reconcile cooperation with a view based on such general oppositions. The 'good vs. bad' approach certainly holds sway in cultural studies and perhaps in the humanities in general, to the extent that the desirability of cooperation survives only in economics and some forms of derived sociology. The challenge is to find a space that could in some way be shared by both realist opposition and the chances for cooperation.

Those who would use translation to save the world in various ways express ambitions that are direct and apparently automatic: translation is so immediately powerful that the translator's choices affect everything else. Look closely at the formulations: they go from the *production* of translations straight to the huge social or cultural effects, as if it were enough to produce a text for it to do something in the world. Production, however, is at best half the story. You have to reach someone who will engage in and interpret your work, and who will then hopefully act in the world. You need active readers. When your intended implicatures fail and you lose credibility as a translator ("Is this guy for real?"), then your translations are unlikely to have much effect in the world.

It is in the space of reception that both realist and cooperative approaches have much to learn. It is there that translators must think carefully about taking risks and seeking corresponding success.

Admiratio

Let me take a step back, actually to one of my least favorite philosophers. In *Les Passions de l'âme* (1649), Descartes describes how all the passions are opposed to each other (love vs. hate, happiness vs. sadness, etc.) except for the first, which he calls *admiration*, from the Latin *admiratio*, sometimes translated as 'wonderment':

> When, upon first encounter, an object surprises us and we esteem it new or quite different from whatever we knew before, or from what we supposed it should be, then we wonder at it and we are astonished by it. And given that this can happen before we know whether this object suits us or not, I think this kind of *admiratio* is the first of all the passions. It has no opposite, since if the object had nothing that surprised us, we would not be moved by it and we would observe it without passion. (Descartes 1649: 82–83; my translation)

I am not sure there is no opposite, given that indifference exists – although one might always argue that it is the absence of passion and thus off the table. The message is nevertheless clear: to foster cooperation across languages and cultures, or indeed to advance the cause of an unfamiliar set of values, it is not enough to ensure safe, risk-averse communication. One also needs to draw attention to the other, using intercultural communication as a series of events able to create *admiratio*, active curiosity, perhaps understandable as the basic question, 'What is this all about?' And if there is to be continued attention, one requires more than a simple note of discord that can easily be dismissed as egoism. Some intelligent risk-taking is required.

The basic argument against risk aversion is easy to make. When texts in the European Commission institutions, for example, are written to be translated, and when the translations all have equal validity, the result is an anodyne discourse that may gain points for clarity but fails to inspire anything like active engagement. That is fair enough for the regulations and directives, since a multilingual polity needs access to clear and accurate laws in all its languages – I do not want to mess with the law. But all the other documents, especially those that concern the ways policies are developed and ideas are discussed, do little to ensure that all citizens feel they are "authors of the laws to which they are subject" (Habermas 1995: 130). That is not to say it is good or bad to want to be European. I merely offer a convenient example of a translation-based communicative regime that inculcates institutional boredom and hence nonparticipation. Most of the 'translation tendencies,' as Levý called them, are found in abundance; few readers could confuse the discourse with lived experience. Something like this critique seems to be behind Christiane Nord's (2014) call for "more courage" in translation – stop being boring!

Since I am trying to address many forms of translation and interpreting here, I hesitate to offer any revolutionary manifesto that might go beyond a general call to pay serious attention to what happens in the space of reception. I have no neat avant-garde to offer: there are simply too many specific types of translation and too many different purposes to seek. The lesson of *admiratio* is much simpler: attract attention to the values of the foreign, then seek cooperation from there.

What might successful risk-taking look like? Examples are not hard to find in promotional discourse, publicity, and film adaptations. Other instances are closer to literalism and transcription, perhaps dating from the kind used from the twelfth century to translate Arabic science into Latin (Pym 2014). And I would include the examples given in the 'risk-taking' section above – excluding those attributed to stupidity. Here I pick up a few further clues from two translators I have known as colleagues.

The Catalan translator Joaquim Mallafrè, who passed away in 2024, has left us a masterful version of Joyce's *Ulysses*. The full range of discourses in Catalan are drawn upon, following the lead of Joyce's playful work on the numerous discourses of popular Dublin and literary tradition. The risk-averse tendencies that make most translations linguistically poorer than their originals are not to be found in Mallafrè's version. Indeed, they are sometimes reversed. Where Joyce brings up a popular saying like, "It's as uncertain as a child's bottom," Mallafrè finds a Catalan expression that is more culturally specific: "És insegur com el cul del Jaumet" – 'as uncertain as Jaimie's bottom' (Mallafrè 2008: 80), and so on. More telling perhaps is the translator's naming of Dublin Castle, the seat of British domination of the city. A *castle* in English normally corresponds to a *castell* in Catalan, and no special risk need be involved. Mallafrè, though, renders it as *ciutadella*, which is not only correct but is also the name of what was the Spanish military stronghold in Barcelona from the eighteenth century (Mallafrè 1991: 61). The translation implicitly maps the British domination of Dublin onto the Spanish domination of Barcelona, inviting an engaged re-interpretation of the entire novel.

Something like this courage is occasionally shown by the British translator John Minford in his versions of the classics of Chinese literature. In his work on *Hong Lou Meng* with David Hawkes, Minford adopted the risk-taking strategies of enlivening scenes and varying not just lexical choices but also languages and literary allusions. I have mentioned Hawkes' use of French and Latin for the names of Chinese characters as being high-risk and not overwhelmingly successful, to judge from readers' online comments. In his own translations, Minford is a little more restrained but no less playful. In his version of the *I Ching* (2015), for example, occasional sayings from ancient Chinese are rendered in Latin, to convey the sense of austerity, and the translated commentaries include one that is full of practical advice for contemporary businesses. These kinds of strategies create a certain *admiratio* in ways that authorized translations from the People's Republic of China often do not – Minford is accused of commercializing classical literature, but he is also bringing texts to life. I am by no means sure that risk-taking will bring about major changes in the world, but I did believe in Minford's translated *I Ching* enough to use it to make a very important decision, which turned out to be a good one.

As a third example of risk-taking, let me mention the work of the Iranian translator, thinker, and activist Omid Tofighian, known for his work on Behrouz Boochani's *No Friend But the Mountains. Writing from Manus Prison* (2018). The original text was written in Persian on WhatsApp and smuggled out of the offshore detention center where the author was imprisoned as a refugee after attempting to enter Australia. Tofighian (2025) recounts how he translated the text into English in collaboration with Boochani, added explanatory material, and promoted the work in Australia, participating in public events and speaking in his own voice in addition to his role as a translator. All of this has involved several very different kinds of risk, including that of usurping the voice of the author (not everyone believes translators should do more than translate), complicating academic employment in Australia (although reasoned activism can also be an asset), and a series of incidents such as the publication of a censored version in Iran (not all the risks are taken on the target side). The work has nevertheless successfully enhanced public awareness of the treatment of refugees and asylum seekers, winning several literary prizes in Australia. Tofighian offers far more than clever theory and a few out-of-place expressions: his is an ongoing lived experience, spreading the work of translation across many discourses and several media.

These kinds of risk-taking are being made easier by the changing landscape of electronic media. Online publication is cheap, opening huge possibilities for retranslations and otherwise variant versions, challenging the institutional illusion of *the* professional translator and *the* one valid translation. When there are several purposes in play, it is possible to translate differently for each and to experiment for all. It is easier now to take very specific risks in search of new kinds of rewards.

What Is to Be Done?

Much as my purpose has been to account for certain things that happen in and around the practice of translation, the risk-management frame can also lead to a few general recommendations concerning future actions and trends. Here is a shortlist:

Teach the risks of automation: Anyone who works with languages must learn to identify the risks and virtues of automated translation, in which I include machine translation and generative AI. This should ideally happen as a part of the foreign-language class, since that is where students are using automation for themselves anyway (see the recommendations in Pym & Hao 2024). The use of automation in class should, of course, point out the fallibility of the systems and the special hazards they incur. To do this, make sure you test how the technologies function when translating into the students' first language, ideally after they have completed an unaided translation. At the same time, automation should also be appreciated and exploited as a source of suggestions, some of which are more inspired than others, about how to make a translation more appealing and engaging. This is where the technologies can help us become more adventurous.

Accept that the basic skills of translation have been democratized: When working with automation, the main comparison is not between the machine and the human, or between the machine translation and the results of generative AI. The important underlying comparison must be between a restrictive profession and the democratization of that profession's basic skills. We must accept that the vast majority of translations in the world are not being done by human professionals. There are serious ecological limitations on how far free public use of the technologies can go (Pym & Hao 2024: 161), but for most everyday purposes, the short-term risks incurred by automation are currently of less consequence than would be the costs of employing a human translator.

Focus on high-stakes situations: It follows from the above that human translators are required in situations where the risks of automation do outweigh the benefits. That rough calculation kicks in whenever the consequences of error are serious, in whatever terms: hazardous outcomes, public image, loss of sales, lack of user participation, impairment of transcendent values (aesthetic or religious), in addition to the noble save-the-world aims. Recognition and fair compensation for our work are most likely in scenarios where the accuracy and quality of translations significantly impact outcomes. That is by no means always the case.

Provide the trustworthiness that automation does not offer: Once you accept the democratization of our basic skills, the task is to identify where human professionals can make meaningful contributions. The obvious option is in the skilled use of the technologies themselves. A second option, closely related, is the verification, correction, and certification of the results, much as is happening already with postediting practices today. As mentioned, the trusted translator should thereby become something akin to the notary who is paid to certify the validity of documents. Translators can certify the validity of translations, as an application of thin trust.

Seek creative transformation: A second pathway that opens in response to automation is to excel in the areas where the technologies do not perform well, particularly in marketing, transcreation, adaptation, and the creation of new content – the general practice of nonliteral translation. The strategies involve risk-taking almost by definition. As I have argued, this pathway runs counter to the way risk management has been handled by professionalization processes in recent history; it requires more than the thin kind of trust that supports the notary function; it assumes the translator can have access to full information concerning readerships and purposes.

Develop thick-trust relations where possible: If and when one desires to move toward that more creative pole of translation, it would make sense to become known to your communication partners on as many levels as possible: as an individual with a past and with aspirations, as someone who can do more than translate, as someone who can be trusted for personal as well as professional reasons. Along this pathway, the more visible you become and the more you can show past success, the more your partners will have reason to trust your decisions.

All these recommendations assume a world where risk is the general condition: there are few clearly understood relations between cause and consequence, and uncertainty is the point of departure for any decision. The tools and models of risk management nevertheless help us understand how we can act in that world, and hopefully, when the aim is long-term cooperation, how we can act better.

References

Abdallah, K. and Koskinen, K. (2007). Managing Trust: Translating and the Network Economy. *Meta* 52(4), 673–687.

Akerlof, G. (1970). The Market for Lemons: Quality Uncertainty and the Market Mechanism. *Quarterly Journal of Economics* 84(3), 488–500.

Allaby, E. (2018). Are Eritrea Government Spies Posing as Refugee Interpreters? *Al Jazeera*, February 26. www.aljazeera.com/features/2018/2/26/are-eritrea-government-spies-posing-as-refugee-interpreters.

Blum-Kulka, S. (1986). Shifts of Cohesion and Coherence in Translation. In J. House and S. Blum-Kulka, eds., *Interlingual and Intercultural Communication*. Tübingen: Narr, pp. 17–35.

Blum-Kulka, S. and Levenston, E. A. (1983). Universals of Lexical Simplification. In C. Faerch and G. Casper, eds., *Strategies in Interlanguage Communication*. London: Longman, pp. 119–139.

Boochani, B. (2019). *No Friend but the Mountains: Writing from Manus Prison*, translated by O. Tofighian, Sydney: Picador.

Bruni, L. (1405/1969). Praefatio in Vita M. Antonii ex Plutarcho traducta. In H. Baron, ed., *Leonardo Bruni Aretino: Humanistisch-philosophische Schriften mit einer Chronologie seiner Werke und Briefe*. 2nd ed. Stuttgart: Teubner, pp. 102–104.

Cadwell, P. (2019). Trust, Distrust and Translation in a Disaster. *Disaster Prevention and Management: An International Journal* 29(2), 157–174.

Canfora, C. and Ottmann, A. (2015). Risikomanagement für Übersetzungen. *trans-kom* 8(2), 314–346.

Canfora, C. and Ottmann, A. (2018). Of Ostriches, Pyramids, and Swiss Cheese – Risks in Safety-Critical Translations. *Translation Spaces* 7(2), 167–201.

Canfora, C. and Ottmann, A. (2020). Risks in Neural Machine Translation. *Translation Spaces* 9(1), 58–77.

Chan, A. L. J. (2008). *Information Economics, the Translation Profession and Translator Certification*. Doctoral thesis. Universitat Rovira i Virgili. http://tdx.cat/handle/10803/8772.

Chesterman, A. (1997). *Memes of Translation: The Spread of Ideas in Translation Theory*. Amsterdam : John Benjamins.

Chesterman, A. and Arrojo, R. (2000). Shared Ground in Translation Studies. *Target* 12(1), 151–160.

References

Church, K. and Hovy, E. (1993). Good Applications for Crummy Machine Translation. *Machine Translation* 8(4), 239–258.

Descartes, R. (1649). *Les Passions de l'âme*. Paris: Henry Le Gras.

Deul, J. (2021). Opinie: Een witte vertaler voor poëzie van Amanda Gorman: onbegrijpelijk. *De Volkskrant*, February 25. www.volkskrant.nl/columns-opinie/opinie-een-witte-vertaler-voor-poezie-van-amanda-gorman-onbegrijpelijk~bf128ae4/.

Dollmann, E. (1967). *The Interpreter: Memoirs of Doktor Eugen Dollmann*. Translated by J. M. Brownjohn. London: Hutchinson.

ELIS Research (2024). *European Language Industry Survey 2024: Trends, Expectations and Concerns of the European Language Industry*. https://elis-survey.org.

Fiedler, S. and Wohlfarth, A. (2018). Language Choices and Practices of Migrants in Germany: An Interview Study. *Language Problems and Language Planning* 42(3), 267–287.

Foster, G. and Frijters, P. (2022). *Hiding the Elephant: The Tragedy of COVID Policy and Its Economist Apologists*. Bonn: IZA – Institute of Labor Economics. https://docs.iza.org/dp15294.pdf.

Frege, G. (1979). Logic. In H. Hermes, F. Kambartel, and F. Kaulback, eds. *Posthumous Writings*, translated by P. Long and R. White. Oxford: Blackwell, pp. 1–8.

Gile, D. (2021). Risk Management in Translation: How Much Does It Really Explain? *International Journal of Interpreter Education* 13(1), 56–65.

Gorman, A. (2021). *The Hill We Climb*. New York: Viking.

Gouadec, D. (2007). *Translation as a Profession*. Amsterdam: John Benjamins.

Granovetter, M. S. (1973). The Strength of Weak Ties. *American Journal of Sociology* 78(6), 1360–1380.

Grice, H. P. (1975). Logic and Conversation. In P. Cole and J. L. Morgan, eds. *Syntax and Semantics*, Vol. 3. New York: Academic Press, pp. 41–58.

Gutt, E. A. (1991). *Translation and Relevance: Cognition and Context*. Oxford: Blackwell.

Habermas, J. (1995). Reconciliation through the Public use of Reason: Remarks on John Rawls's Political Liberalism. *The Journal of Philosophy* 92(3), 109–131.

Hajek, J., Karidakis, M., Amorati, R. et al. (2022). *Understanding the Experiences and Communication Needs of Culturally and Linguistically Diverse Communities during the COVID-19 Pandemic*. Report prepared for the Victorian Department of Families, Fairness and Housing. Melbourne: Research Unit for Multilingualism and Cross-Cultural Communication, University of Melbourne.

Hajek, J., Pym, A., Hao, Y. et al. (2024). *Understanding and Improving Machine Translations for Emergency Communications*. Report prepared for the Victorian Department of Families, Fairness and Housing. Melbourne: Research Unit for Multilingualism and Cross-Cultural Communication, University of Melbourne. https://doi.org/10.17613/jthe-m639.

Halverson, S. and Kotze, H. (2022). Sociocognitive Constructs in Translation and Interpreting Studies (TIS). In S. L. Halverson and Á. Marín García, eds., *Contesting Epistemologies in Cognitive Translation and Interpreting Studies*. Abingdon: Routledge, pp. 51–79.

Hansson, H. (2022). Gurnah x 2: Översättning som extremsport. *Med andra ord* 110, 23–26.

Harari, Y. N. (2014). *Sapiens: A Brief History of Humankind*. London: Harvill Secker.

Harari, Y. N. (2016). *Homo deus: A Brief History of Tomorrow*. London: Harvill Secker.

Harrison, B. G. (1994). Once in Love with Giorgio. *New York Times Book Review* 21 August 8.

Hjort, M. (2017). Affect, Risk Management and the Translation of Swearing. *Rask. Internationalt tidsskrift for sprog og kommunikation* 46, 159–180.

Hönig, H. G. and P. Kussmaul (1982). *Strategie der Übersetzung: Ein Lehr- und Arbeitsbuch*. Tübingen: Narr.

Hosking, G. (2014). *Trust: A History*. Oxford: Oxford University Press.

Hu, B. (2020). How are Translation Norms Negotiated? A Case Study of Risk Management in Chinese Institutional Translation. *Target* 32(1), 83–121. https://doi.org/10.1075/target.19050.hu.

Hu, B. (2022). Feeling Foreign: A Trust-based Compromise Model of Translation Reception. *Translation Studies* 15(2), 202–220. https://doi.org/10.1080/14781700.2022.2032306.

Hui, M. (2012). *Risk Management by Translator Trainees: A Study of Translator-Client Relations in a Simulated Setting*. Doctoral thesis. Universitat Rovira i Virgili. www.tdx.cat/handle/10803/83497.

ISO (2018). *Risk Management – Guidelines. ISO31000:2018*. www.iso.org/obp/ui/#iso:std:iso:31000:ed-2:v1:en.

Ju, E. M. (2009). The Professionalization of Interpreting in Taiwan: A Critical Review of Tseng's Model. *Compilation and Translation Review* 2(2), 105–125.

Kahneman, D. (2011). *Thinking, Fast and Slow*. New York: Farrar, Straus and Giroux.

Klaudy, K. (1993). On Explicitation Hypothesis. In K. Klaudy and J. Kohn, eds., *Transferre necesse est ... Current Issues of Translation Theory*. Szombathely: Daniel Berzsenyi College, pp. 69–77.

Koskinen, K. (2008). *Translating Institutions: An Ethnographic Study of EU Translation*. Manchester: St Jerome.

Lafeber, A. (2022). Translator Training at United Nations Headquarters, New York. In T. Svoboda, Ł. Biel and V. Sosoni, eds., *Institutional Translator Training*. New York: Routledge, pp. 234–243.

Lammers, M. (2011). Risk Management in Localization. In K. J. Dunne and E. S. Dunne, eds., *Translation and Localization Project Management: The Art of the Possible*. Amsterdam: John Benjamins, pp. 211–232.

Leonard, S. (2005). Progress against the law. Anime and fandom, with the key to the globalization of culture. *International Journal of Cultural Studies* 8(3), 281–305.

Lesznyák, Á. (2019). Hungarian Translators' Perceptions of Neural Machine Translation in the European Commission. In M. Forcada, A. Way, B. Haddow and R. Sennrich, eds., *Proceedings of Machine Translation Summit XVII*. Dublin: European Association for Machine Translation, pp. 16–22.

Lewicki, R. J., McAllister, D. J., and Bies, R. J. (1998). Trust and Distrust: New Relationships and Realities. *The Academy of Management Review* 23(3), 438–458.

Levý, J. (1963/2011) *Umění překladu*, translated by P. Corness, ed. Z. Jettmarová, as *The Art of Translation*. Amsterdam: John Benjamins.

Luhmann, N. (1968). *Vertrauen: Ein Mechanismus der Reduktion sozialer Komplexität*. Amsterdam: Ferdinand Enke.

Luhmann, N. (1988). Familiarity, Confidence, Trust: Problems and Alternatives. In D. Gambetta, ed., *Trust Making and Breaking: Cooperative Relations*. Oxford: Blackwell, pp. 94–108.

Lyu, C., Xu, J. and Wang, L. (2023). New Trends in Machine Translation using Large Language Models: Case Examples with ChatGPT. https://arxiv.org/pdf/2305.01181.pdf.

Macklovitch, E. (1984). Recent Canadian Experience in Machine Translation. Conference on *Methodology and Techniques of Machine Translation*. British Computer Society. https://aclanthology.org/1984.bcs-1.31.pdf.

Macreadie, R., Bouyzourn, K., Meylaerts, R. and Pym, A. (2025). Thick and Thin Trust in Translated Cross-Cultural Vaccination Messaging. In B. Hu, S. Valdez and V. Ragni, eds., *(De)constructing trust in high-stakes intercultural communication: Theoretical, methodological and practical challenges*, Special issue of *Translation Studies*.

Mallafrè, J. (1991). *Llengua de tribu i llengua de polis: Bases d'una traducció literària*. Barcelona: Quaderns Crema.

Mallafrè, J. (2008). Translating Ulysses. *Papers on Joyce* 14, 71–83.

Malmkjær, K. (1997). Punctuation in Hans Christian Andersen's Stories and in their Translations into English. In F. Poyatos, ed., *Nonverbal Communication and Translation*. Amsterdam: Benjamins, pp. 151–162.

Malmkjær, K. (2005). Norms and Nature in Translation Studies. *Synaps: Fagspråk, Kommuniksjon, Kulturkunnscap* 16, 13–19.

Matsushita, K. (2016). *Risk Management in the Decision-Making Process of English-Japanese News Translation*. Doctoral thesis. Rikkyo University, Tokyo.

Minford, J., trans. (2015). *I Ching (Yijing). The Book of Change*. New York: Penguin.

Möllering, G. (2001). The Nature of Trust: From Georg Simmel to a Theory of Expectation, Interpretation and Suspension. *Sociology* 35(2), 403–420. https://doi.org/10.1017/S0038038501000190.

Monacelli, C. and Punzo, R. (2001). Ethics in the Fuzzy Domain of Interpreting: A "Military" Perspective. *The Translator* 7(2), 265–282.

Nord, C. (2014). *Hürden-Sprünge: Ein Plädoyer für mehr Mut beim Übersetzen*. Berlin: BDÜ Weiterbildungs- und Fachverlagsgesellschaft.

PEN America (2023). The 2023 Manifesto on Literary Translation. https://pen.org/report/translation-manifesto/.

Putnam, R. D. (2000). *Bowling Alone: The Collapse and Revival of American Community*. New York: Simon and Schuster.

Pokorn, N. K. and Čibej, J. (2018). Interpreting and Linguistic Inclusion – Friends or Foes? Results from a Field Study. *The Translator* 24(2), 111–127.

Pym, A. (1993). *Epistemological Problems in Translation and its Teaching*. Calaceite: Caminade.

Pym, A. (1995). Translation as a Transaction Cost. *Meta* 40(4), 594–605.

Pym, A. (2007). On Shlesinger's Proposed Equalizing Universal for Interpreting. In F. Pöchhacker, A. Lykke Jakobsen, and I. M. Mees, eds., *Interpreting Studies and beyond: A Tribute to Miriam Shlesinger*. Copenhagen: Samfundslitteratur Press, pp. 175–190.

Pym, A. (2008). On Omission in Simultaneous Interpreting: Risk Analysis of a Hidden Effort. In G. Hansen, A. Chesterman, and H. Gerzymisch-Arbogast, eds., *Efforts and Models in Interpreting and Translation Research*. Amsterdam: John Benjamins, pp. 83–105.

Pym, A. (2014). *Negotiating the Frontier: Translators and Intercultures in Hispanic History*. Abingdon: Routledge.

Pym, A. (2016). Risk Analysis as a Heuristic Tool in the Historiography of Interpreters: For an Understanding of Worst Practices. In J. Baigorri-Jalón and K. Takeda, eds., *New Insights in the History of Interpreting*. Amsterdam: John Benjamins, pp. 247–268.

Pym, A. (2020). Translation, Risk Management and Cognition. In A. Lykke Jakobsen and F. Alves, eds., *The Routledge Handbook of Translation and Cognition*. Abingdon: Routledge, pp. 445–458.

Pym, A. (2022). Who Says who Interprets? On the Possible Existence of an Interpreter System. *The Translator* 28(2), 162–177. https://doi.org/10.1080/13556509.2022.2083752.

Pym, A. (2023a). *Exploring Translation Theories*. 3rd ed.. Abingdon: Routledge.

Pym, A. (2023b). Triage and Technology in Healthcare Translation. In G. Palumbo, K. Peruzzo, and G. Pontrandolfo, eds., *What's Special about Specialised Translation?* Bern: Peter Lang. pp. 247–268.

Pym, A. and Hao, Y. (2024). *Augmenting Language Skills: Generative AI and Machine Translation in Language Learning and Translator Training*. Abingdon: Routledge.

Pym, A. and Hu, B. (2022). Trust and Cooperation through Social Media. COVID-19 Translations for Chinese Communities in Melbourne. In T. K. Lee and D. Wang, eds., *Translation and Social Media Communication in the Age of the Pandemic*. Abingdon: Routledge, pp. 44–61.

Pym, A. and Hu, K. (2024). Trade-offs in Translation Effects: Illustrations and Methodological Concerns. *Target*. https://doi.org/10.1075/target.23010.pym.

Pym, A. and Matsushita, K. (2018). Risk Mitigation in Translator Decisions. *Across Languages and Cultures* 19(1), 1–18. https://doi.org/10.1556/084.2018.19.1.1.

Pym, A. and Torres-Simón, E. (2021). Is Automation Changing the Translation Profession?. *International Journal of the Sociology of Language* 270, 39–57. https://doi.org/10.1515/ijsl-2020-0015.

Pym, A., Grin, F., Sfreddo, C. and Chan, A. L. J. (2013). *The Status of the Translation Profession in the European Union*. Luxembourg: European Commission.

Pym, A., Raigal-Aran, J. and Bestué Salinas, C. (2023). Non-standard Court Interpreting as Risk Management. In C. Zwischenberger, K. Reithofer and S. Rennert, eds., *Introducing New Hypertexts on Interpreting (Studies)*. Amsterdam: John Benjamins, pp. 107–124.

Qiu, J. (2024). The Presence of Source Viewership in Fansub Paratexts. *Translation and Translanguaging in Multilingual Contexts* 10(1), 54–73.

Qiu, J. and Pym, A. (2024). Fatal Flaws? Investigating the Effects of Machine Translation Errors on Audience Reception in the Audiovisual Context. *Perspectives. Studies in Translation Theory and Practice*. https://doi.org/10.1080/0907676X.2024.2328757.

References

Racó català (2004). Aneu amb compte amb la traducció del llibre el codi da vinci. www.racocatala.cat/forums/fil/1024/.

Rizzi, A., Lang, B., and Pym, A. (2019). *What Is Translation History? A Trust-based Approach*. Cham: Palgrave Macmillan.

Robinson, D. (2023). *Questions for Translation Studies*. Amsterdam: John Benjamins.

Samir, A. (2024). A Comparative Study of Translation Strategies for Taboo Words in Persian Translations of Contemporary American Self-help Literature. *International Journal of Religion* 5(11), 1723–1740. https://doi.org/10.61707/9aa0n242.

Sapiro, G. (2014). Translation as a Weapon in the Struggle against Cultural Hegemony in the Era of Globalization. *Bibliodiversity* 3, 31–40.

Sapiro, G. (2019). Translation and Translation as a Weapon. *Oxford Research Encyclopedia of Literature*. https://doi.org/10.1093/acrefore/9780190201098.013.942.

Senmache Artola, D. N. (2019). *Análisis de los errores en la traducción al español del libro "El Código Da Vinci" del escritor Dan Brown*. Tesis de Licenciatura. Lima: Universidad Ricardo Palma.

Shlesinger, M. (1989). *Simultaneous Interpretation as a Factor in Effecting Shifts in the Position of Texts on the Oral-Literate Continuum*. MA thesis, Tel Aviv University. https://doi.org/10.13140/RG.2.2.31471.69285.

Smith, A. (1776/2000). *The Wealth of Nations*. New York: Random House.

Stoeller, W. (2003). Risky Business: Risk Management for Localization Project Managers. www.translationdirectory.com/article462.htm.

Sudhoff, K. (1909). Planta noctis. *Archiv für Geschichte der Medezin* 3 (4–5), 352.

Suojanen, T., Koskinen, K. and Tuominen, T. (2015). *User-Centered Translation*. London: Routledge.

Sztompka, P. (1997). *Trust, Distrust and the Paradox of Democracy*. WZB Discussion Paper No. P 97-003. Wissenschaftszentrum Berlin für Sozialforschung.

Takeda, K. (2010). *Interpreting the Tokyo War Crimes Tribunal: A Sociopolitical Analysis*. Ottawa: University of Ottawa Press.

Tarchetti, I. U. (1994). *Passion*. Translated by L. Venuti. San Francisco: Mercury House.

Tofighian, O. (2025). *Creating New Languages of Resistance: Translation, Public Philosophy and Border Violence*. Abingdon: Routledge.

Tomter, L., Zondag, M. H. W. and Skille, Ø. B. (2017). Warning about Translation Web Site: Passwords and Contracts Accessible on the Internet.

NRK, September 3. www.nrk.no/urix/warning-about-translation-web-site_-passwords-and-contracts-accessible-on-the-internet-1.13670874.

Toury, G. (2012). *Descriptive Translation Studies and beyond*. 2nd ed. Amsterdam: John Benjamins.

Vanderauwera, R. (1985). *Dutch Novels Translated into English: The Transformation of a "Minority" Literature*. Amsterdam: Rodopi.

Vandevoorde, L. and Lefever, E. (2023). Who's Afraid of False Friends? Cognate Ratios in Translated and Non-translated Dutch. *Across Languages and Cultures* 24(1), 73–84. https://doi.org/10.1556/084.2022.00204.

Vazquez-Ayora, G. (1977). *Introducción a la traductología: Curso básico de traducción*. Washington, DC: Georgetown University Press.

Venuti, L. (1994). Introduction. I. U. Tarchetti, *Passion*. San Francisco: Mercury House, pp. v–xvi.

Venuti, L. (1998). *The Scandals of Translation: Towards an Ethics of Difference*. Abingdon: Routledge.

Wang, A. and Liu, K. (2024). Linguistic Variations between Translated and Non-Translated English Chairman's Statements in Corporate Annual Reports: A Multidimensional Analysis. *Sage Open*. https://doi.org/10.1177/21582440241249349.

Weiser, B. (2023). Here's What Happens When Your Lawyer Uses ChatGPT. *The New York Times*, May 27. https://www.nytimes.com/2023/05/27/nyregion/avianca-airline-lawsuit-chatgpt.html.

Acknowledgments

I have been playing with risk management as an approach to translation since 2003, when I started giving talks on how it could remove the need for equivalence as a concept in translation theory. I started arguing that a translation is not wrong because it is nonequivalent, but because it increases the probabilities of communicative failure. And the greater the probability of failure, the more it is wrong. At the time, this was a commonsensical attempt to formalize the ideas of *Skopos* theory. As I worked on the ideas, further concepts came to enrich the approach, especially cooperation as communicative success, and then trust as the social glue necessary for cooperative relationships over time. Risk management has now hopefully become a little more than a commonsensical formulation, especially if it can help us work with new technologies.

The development of the approach has benefited from numerous empirical applications, many of them in the form of doctoral theses that I supervised. Andy Lung Jan Chan (2008) applied the theory of adverse selection to the translation market, showing the risks of uncertain signals of quality. Work with François Grin and Claudio Sfreddo further developed the approach as an analysis of the status of translators in the European Union (Pym, Grin, Sfreddo, & Chan 2013). Maggie Hui (2012) applied risk management to an entire classroom activity simulating translator-client relations, developing ways of describing the risk profile of each participant. In Tokyo, Kayo Matsushita (2015) and her supervisor Kayoko Takeda went well beyond my initial forays in her work on English-Japanese news translation. In Melbourne, Bei Hu and I analyzed the United States' 'One China' policy in terms of strategically non-corresponding translations, before Bei applied the general risk-management approach to the translation of foreign-affairs discourse in China and its reception in Australia. With Bei and then Ke Hu, we added trade-off models to the conceptual arsenal and then Ke and I used them to describe the reception of literary translations (Pym and Hu 2024). In Melbourne, I have been very pleased to work with Andrea Rizzi and Birgit Lang on trust as an approach to translation history (Rizzi, Lang, & Pym 2019), where risk as such remains in the shadows but is an important shadow. In parallel, work with Judith Raigal Aran in Tarragona and Carmen Bestué Salinas in Barcelona has used risk analysis and trust to analyze recordings of court proceedings, in particular throwing light on some of the more spectacular ways trust can be lost.

Two recent events have given fresh impetus to this work on risk management. The COVID years brought the logics of risks and trade-offs into headlines across the globe, particularly when translations of medical information met with significant delays, limited understanding, and instances of low social trust. In Melbourne, Bei Hu and I studied those dynamics in some detail (Pym & Hu 2022) and I participated in a major interview study on the ways healthcare information was received and processed in ethnic-specific communities (Hajek et al. 2022). The second event would then comprise public discourse on generative AI since 2022. This has filled headlines with all kinds of perceived and often imagined risks, which some of us have sought to address empirically: risk analysis has been central to our group work in Melbourne on the use of machine translation for emergency messaging (Hajek et al. 2024) and plays an important role in the research Yu Hao and I have done on the teaching of machine translation and generative AI (Pym & Hao 2024).

I give this list not only to thank all those excellent scholars but also to indicate the very varied empirical research that lies behind the theory – in addition to all the linguistic research on the ways the language in translations differs from the language in non-translations (which I interpret as indices of general risk aversion among translators). Examples from most of these projects are given throughout this text. I also list the projects to make it clear that, although I tend to cite high-stakes cases like bushfire emergencies, risk management can be applied to all kinds of translation, in all genres.

I have enjoyed wonderful working relationships with all those people. We have long shared a sense of discovering new things, opening new territory, and experimenting with new ways to apply what are basically ideas from economics and psychology to the practice of cross-cultural communication. Risk management can explain data that other theories struggle with, particularly when it comes to the reasons why translators make certain choices in certain situations. The approach nevertheless remains a minority sport. It has perhaps been stranded between the hyper-empirical (all the detailed corpus and process studies on what happens in translation) and the hyper-ideological (all the save-the-world studies on what can or should happen because of translations). To connect those two extremes, someone might still want to know *why* translators might make decisions one way or the other, and *how* people interpret and use translations in specific situations, including when saving the world. If so, we have a few ideas that you are invited to explore.

Cambridge Elements

Translation and Interpreting

The series is edited by Kirsten Malmkjær with Sabine Braun as associate editor for Elements focusing on Interpreting.

Kirsten Malmkjær
University of Leicester

Kirsten Malmkjær is Professor Emeritus of Translation Studies at the University of Leicester. She has taught Translation Studies at the universities of Birmingham, Cambridge, Middlesex and Leicester and has written extensively on aspects of both the theory and practice of the discipline. *Translation and Creativity* (London: Routledge) was published in 2020 and *The Cambridge Handbook of Translation*, which she edited, was published in 2022. She is preparing a volume entitled *Introducing Translation* for the Cambridge Introductions to Language and Linguistics series.

Editorial Board
Adriana Serban, *Université Paul Valéry*
Barbara Ahrens, *Technische Hochschule Köln*
Liu Min-Hua, *Hong Kong Baptist University*
Christine Ji, *The University of Sydney*
Jieun Lee, *Ewha Womans University*
Lorraine Leeson, *The University of Dublin*
Sara Laviosa, *Università Delgi Stuidi di Bari Aldo Moro*
Fabio Alves, *FALE-UFMG*
Moira Inghilleri, *University of Massachusetts Amherst*
Akiko Sakamoto, *University of Portsmouth*
Haidee Kotze, *Utrecht University*

About the Series

Elements in Translation and Interpreting present cutting edge studies on the theory, practice and pedagogy of translation and interpreting. The series also features work on machine learning and AI, and human-machine interaction, exploring how they relate to multilingual societies with varying communication and accessibility needs, as well as text-focused research.

Cambridge Elements

Translation and Interpreting

Elements in the Series

On-Screen Language in Video Games
Mikołaj Deckert and Krzysztof W. Hejduk

Navigating the Web
Claire Y. Shih

The Graeco-Arabic Translation Movement
El-Hussein AY Aly

Interpreting as Translanguaging
Lili Han, Zhisheng (Edward) Wen and Alan James Runcieman

Creative Classical Translation
Paschalis Nikolaou

Translation as Creative–Critical Practice
Delphine Grass

Translation in Analytic Philosophy
Francesca Ervas

Towards Game Translation User Research
Mikołaj Deckert, Krzysztof W. Hejduk, and Miguel Á. Bernal-Merino

Hypertranslation
Mª Carmen África Vidal Claramonte and Tong King Lee

An Extraordinary Chinese Translation of Holocaust Testimony
Meiyuan Zhao

Researching and Modelling the Translation Process
Muhammad M. M. Abdel Latif

Risk Management in Translation
Anthony Pym

A full series listing is available at: www.cambridge.org/EITI

www.ingramcontent.com/pod-product-compliance
Lightning Source LLC
Chambersburg PA
CBHW050701280125
20949CB00006BA/394